PLANNING AND
DESIGNING
Effective

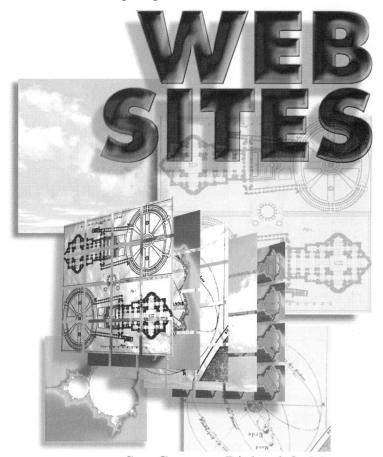

WEB
SITES

Sue Conger • Richard O. Mason

COURSE
TECHNOLOGY

ONE MAIN STREET, CAMBRIDGE, MA 02142

an International Thomson Publishing company I(T)P®

Cambridge • Albany • Bonn • Boston • Cincinnati • London • Madrid • Melbourne • Mexico City
New York • Paris • San Francisco • Singapore • Tokyo • Toronto • Washington

CREDITS:

Managing Editor:	Kristen Duerr	**Composition House:**	GEX, Inc.
Senior Product Manager:	Jennifer Normandin	**Text & Cover Design:**	Efrat Reis
Senior Production Editor:	Catherine G. DiMassa	**Marketing Manager:**	Tracy Foley
Development Editors:	India Koopman, Kim Crowley		

© 1998 by Course Technology— I(T)P®

FOR MORE INFORMATION CONTACT:

Course Technology
One Main Street
Cambridge, MA 02142

ITP Europe
Berkshire House 168-173
High Holborn
London WC1V 7AA
England

Nelson ITP Australia
102 Dodds Street
South Melbourne, 3205
Victoria, Australia

ITP Nelson Canada
1120 Birchmount Road
Scarborough, Ontario
Canada M1K 5G4

International Thomson Editores
Seneca, 53
Colonia Polanco
11560 Mexico D.F. Mexico

ITP GmbH
Knigswinterer Strasse 418
53277 Bonn
Germany

ITP Asia
60 Albert Street, #15-01
Albert Complex
Singapore 189969

ITP Japan
Hirakawacho Kyowa Building, 3F
2-2-1 Hirakawacho
Chiyoda-ku, Tokyo 102
Japan

ISBN: 0-7600-4988-2

Printed in the United States of America
1 2 3 4 5 6 7 8 9 10   01 00 99 98 97

CONTENTS

PREFACE

The World Wide Web is becoming a pervasive—some say invasive—force in our daily lives. We have all seen Web sites that are cleanly designed, pleasing to look at, and helpful as we try to conduct our businesses and our lives as smoothly as we can. For every one of those Web sites, however, we have seen several that are poorly designed, unattractive, and confusing.

The purpose of this book is to show you how to analyze information and apply graphic design techniques to develop effective, pleasing, useful Web sites. The techniques apply equally to intranet, extranet, and Web presentations.

ABOUT THIS BOOK

This book is written primarily for people who intend to design and implement pages for the World Wide Web—that is, anyone who must create a Web site from the vague ideas of those who want to present themselves, their organization, their products, or their services on the Web. However, anyone associated with a World Wide Web project—including those already up and running—can benefit from this text. The techniques and methods presented can and should be applied not only to create an informative, engaging presentation but also to maintain such a presentation.

During both the designing of a site and its upkeep, the key to an effective presentation is the willingness to consistently and repeatedly analyze, evaluate, and improve it, whether by updating or clarifying information, introducing a new technology, or adding or removing hyperlinks to make it easier for the person using the site to move through it. Meeting the needs and wants of that person—the user—should always be the goal.

The book is presented in four parts. Part I, "Behind the Web," provides background information on the World Wide Web and introduces the roles of the four key players involved in the design process: presenters, information stewards, designers, and—of course—Web site users. Each of these parties plays an important role in the success of a Web presentation.

Parts II and III present techniques and methods that lead you step by step from conception of a project through successful design. While presented formally, these techniques and methods can be applied quite informally as well. The approach is useful for large projects with thousands of pages or small projects with only a few pages.

Part II, "Preparation," discusses the steps done in preparation for Web site design. This is when information is gathered and analyzed to determine what should be included in the Web site.

Part III, "Design Methods," takes you through the process of designing Web pages, which involves the writing of text, the arrangement of hyperlinks, and the many uses of multimedia. Techniques from graphic design, photographic composition, and other communication arts are presented in terms of their application to Web site design.

Part IV, "Ongoing Support," describes the activities that go into maintaining a Web site once it is up and running. Again, the key to a successful site is continuous monitoring and improvement.

Of course, no explanation of Web site design would be complete without actual implementation of "live," online pages. Implementation is the focus of the Web Workshop CD-ROM that accompanies the book. The CD has two main sections. The "Web Workshop" section features a tutorial for learning basic HTML (the formatting language of Web pages) and how to use it to design pages. Software called "Editor" then allows you to create, modify, and preview your own Web pages. The Editor includes several samples of Web pages that let you try your hand at customizing design. The second section, "Surfing," provides Web pages and sites that you can critique based on the design concepts presented in the book. This CD does not require Internet access, only a browser such as Netscape Navigator or Microsoft Internet Explorer.

SPECIAL FEATURES

In combination, the book, the CD, and online resources provided by Course Technology on our Web site (www.course.com) provide a number of features that will help you master and apply the knowledge and skills involved in designing and maintaining Web sites.

Features of this package include:

- **The CD-ROM**, which will give you the basics of HTML and take you through CGI/Perl and JavaScript, enable you to practice concepts presented in the text, and help you to develop your own Web pages and sites.

- **A running case study in Web design and implementation**, based on our own consulting experience. Called "Web Design in the Real World," the case begins each chapter and presents the Web design process as it was experienced by one of the fastest-growing small businesses in the United States, portrayed here as the Best Personalized Books company. The work involved in each phase of Web planning and design discussed in the text is demonstrated, chapter by chapter, in the case study.

- **An ongoing case project** in which you plan, design, and implement a Web site.

- **"Go to" boxes** in each chapter of the text that identify Web sites you can visit that effectively apply the design concepts being discussed.

- **Screen shots** of many Web pages throughout the book, plus an 8-page color insert of Web screen shots that demonstrate many of the design concepts discussed.

- **End-of-chapter questions** that test your knowledge of the concepts just presented.

- **End-of-chapter surfing exercises** that allow you to analyze and comment on numerous sites on the World Wide Web, deciding for yourself which are effective, which are not, and why.

- **Icons of a surfer and a spider web** in the end-of chapter material and on the CD that show you where you can go on the CD to complete an exercise or learn more on a given topic.

- **A Web site sponsored by Course Technology** that you can use to find links to other interesting Web sites, corrections of any errors found in the book, and updated information on Web design techniques and technologies.

INSTRUCTOR SUPPORT

In addition, the following instructor support materials are available to accompany this text when it is used in an academic setting:

- An on-line instructor's manual that provides downloadable PowerPoint presentations to accompany each chapter, additional Web sites that are updated twice a semester to provide relevant hyperlinks for each chapter, and answers to the end-of-chapter questions.

- A powerful assessment tool known as Course Test Manager. Designed by Course Technology, this cutting-edge Windows-based testing software helps instructors design and administer tests and pre-tests. In addition to being able to generate tests that can be printed and administered, this full-featured program also has an online testing component that allows students to take tests at the computer and have their exams automatically graded. The test bank that accompanies this text features up to 100 questions per chapter.

ACKNOWLEDGMENTS

We gratefully acknowledge the patience and considerable work of the students in MIS4305 in the fall of 1994, 1995, and 1996 and the students of MIS6310 in spring 1996 who built World Wide Web applications, leading us to develop this book. We also thank the supportive, idea-generating imaginative users for whom the projects were developed and who provided the considerable and impressive basic Web pages from which the much of the work was developed. They include Southern Methodist University faculty and staff Keith Pendergrass, Dee Powell, Ellen Ferris, Blake Ives, Brian Downs, John Grout, Allen Gwinn, Bill May, and Arden Showalter.

The Course Technology staff and editors were all very helpful and understanding of the many problems and personal setbacks we experienced during the writing and editing of the book. They include India Koopman, who translated our academic words into understandable prose and who has to be one of the most patient and best editors alive; Jennifer Normandin, senior product manager, who improved our graphical presentation and kept us on schedule; Kristen Duerr, managing editor, who made this all happen; Catherine DiMassa, production editor, who got us through production; Heidi Schumacher, copy editor, who greatly improved the illustrations and diagrams in the book as well as our English; and Greg Bigelow, who quality-approved the Web Workshop CD.

The work, ideas, and support of Carlos Mendez, who created much of the CD-ROM, greatly improved its content and presentation, and are very much appreciated. We would like to acknowledge the support and helpful comments of Mary Prescott, Richard Vedder, Juhani Iivari, Marshall Hays, George Yedinak, Thane Marston, and Gerald Anderson. Finally, we thank Foxie Mason, the late Dave Conger, Katie Conger, and Lis Nielsen for their incredible patience, which made the book happen.

We apologize to anyone we may have left out. We realize that without continuing support the project would have floundered, and any errors or omissions are our own. We would be grateful for comments and feedback on the use of the methods presented here or on any errors found.

Sue Conger
Richard Mason

Part 1

BEHIND THE WEB

BEHIND THE WEB

The World Wide Web is one of the greatest phenomena of modern time. Individuals and organizations are rushing to gain access to it and to make their presence known on it. Why are they doing this? Who is affected and why? Whose efforts are required to develop a successful Web presentation, and what processes are involved in its creation? This book will give you the answers to these questions. After completing the book and the project assignments, you will have developed your own Web presentation and will understand the complex roles and processes behind an effective Web site.

Chapter 1 introduces you to the World Wide Web and how it is used to share and obtain information. In particular, three criteria of a successful World Wide Web presentation—effectiveness, affectiveness, and navigational efficiency—are discussed. These criteria are the foundation for Web presentation design throughout the book.

Chapter 2 describes the roles of the people behind every World Wide Web presentation—presenter, information steward, designer, and viewer. Each role is defined and its primary Web activities described. The discussion is intended to help all those contributing to the development of a Web site understand their own and others' roles—and to help designers, in particular, manage the relationships between them.

Each chapter begins with a short introduction to the chapter material as it relates to Best Personalized Books, an actual company located in Dallas, Texas. Best Personalized Books develops and sells software used to produce personalized children's books and other products. At the end of each chapter, we will discuss the development of a Web site for Best Personalized Books.

1

Introduction to World Wide Web Presentations

In This Chapter You Will Learn To:

- Describe the overall process by which and for whom Web presentations are developed
- Explain the three essential design criteria in a successful Web presentation and the need for trade-offs among them
- Define an understanding business and explain how mutual understanding is achieved by a Web presentation
- Explain the three potential purposes of a Web presentation—information, entertainment, or persuasion

W e b   D e s i g n   i n   t h e   R e a l   W o r l d

Best Personalized Books

Best Personalized Books is a $6 million company located in Dallas, Texas. The company develops and sells software for producing personalized children's books and other personalized products. The children's book line has 34 titles available in 17 languages and ranges from nonproprietary items such as birthday stories to licensed Disney, NFL, and Power Rangers products. Other products include stationery, books, and novelty items, such as clocks.

Best Personalized Books was started six years ago, literally in the kitchen of the owners, Jack and Wendy Kalisher. The company has since relocated to a 50,000-square-foot facility with more than 70 employees and has a global network with thousands of licensed agents who sell their books. They were recognized as 167th in *Inc. Magazine*'s list of fastest growing small companies in the United States[1] and have received recognition for their success, including a letter from President Bill Clinton.

Best's growth has not lost momentum. Its owners recently decided to use the World Wide Web as a new medium to expand the company.

Introduction to the World Wide Web

Daily, tens of millions of people access trillions of bytes (or characters) of data on the World Wide Web. Commonly called the **Web**, the **World Wide Web** (WWW) is a *structure of documents* connected electronically over the Internet. The **Internet** is a large *computer network* made up of smaller networks and computers all connected electronically. A network consists of two or more computers connected for the purpose of sharing information and resources. At last count, there were more than 16 million computers or more than 50,000 networks connected to the Internet.[2]

Each document on the Web is called a **Web document** or **Web page**. These documents pull together different types of information, including text, graphics, sound, animation, and video. A related set of Web pages is called a **Web presentation,** or **site**. The term "presentation" is used in the book since the term "site" can also refer to several presentations stored on the same computer.

Web presentations are stored on computers, called **Web servers**, which are connected to the Internet. When people access the World Wide Web they use a software program called a **Web browser** that enables them to access, view, and navigate all the documents on the Web. Some of the more common Web browsers available are Mosaic, Microsoft Internet Explorer, and Netscape

1. "The Inc 500: The Fastest-Growing Private Companies," *Inc. Magazine,* December 17, 1995
2. See http://info.ison.org/internet-history/ Timeline.htm

Navigator. Web pages are formatted by these browsers, which interpret a language called **HTML**, or **HyperText Markup Language**, that is embedded in the document. Web browsers recognize HTML codes and use them to format the display as seen on the screen.

Web pages are identified by a unique address called a **Uniform Resource Locator**, or **URL**. The URL specifies where on the Internet a particular resource is stored. These resources include Web pages. Figure 1-1 shows the format of a typical URL address and how each of its components helps to identify the Web page's location on the Internet. Web browsers use URL addresses to locate and access Web page documents and other multimedia objects, such as video clips, on the Web.

http//domain/x/y/z/webpage.html	Typical format for the URL, or address, of a resource on the Internet, including documents on the World Wide Web.
http//www.netscape.com/welcome.html	Example of a URL on the Web. Each component has a distinct meaning, as described below.
http//	The **h**ypertext **t**ransfer **p**rotocol (http), or standard for communication, that governs transfer of several types of Web objects. Another protocol is ftp, or **f**ile **t**ransfer **p**rotocol, which allows files to be downloaded from a particular site to another computer.
www.location.orgtype	This information, which falls under the "domain" category in the typical URL format shown above, identifies the computer where the document is stored. The domain suffix identifies country (as in fi for Finland), organization (.org), school (.edu), government agency (.gov), Internet service provider (.net), commercial enterprise (.com), and so on. The URL translates into a numeric address. The URL www.njit.edu translates as 128.235.163.2.
/x/y/z /	One or more subdirectories, or paths, which identify an exact location on the computer. For instance, /faculty/mis/ points to a "faculty" directory with an "mis" subdirectory.
webpage.html	The last URL entry is the document name that is stored as a **h**ypertext **m**arkup **l**anguage (html) document. In this example, "webpage" is the document name and ".html" is the extension that identifies it as an HTML-formatted document.

Figure 1-1   Interpreting URLs

Once you have accessed a Web page using a Web browser, you can access other documents on the Web by clicking a hyperlink. A **hyperlink** is an address identifying a computer file path name or URL in a Web page that you can click to access another location on the same page, another Web page stored on that Web site, or a Web page stored somewhere else on the Internet. This system of linked information is called **hypertext**. Files containing hyperlinks are called **hyperlink documents**. You click a hyperlink to navigate, or **jump**, to a different document containing related information. The Web pages shown in Figure 1-2 demonstrate examples of hyperlinks both within and between Web presentations for the Mars Shop and the Mars Pathfinder Mission.

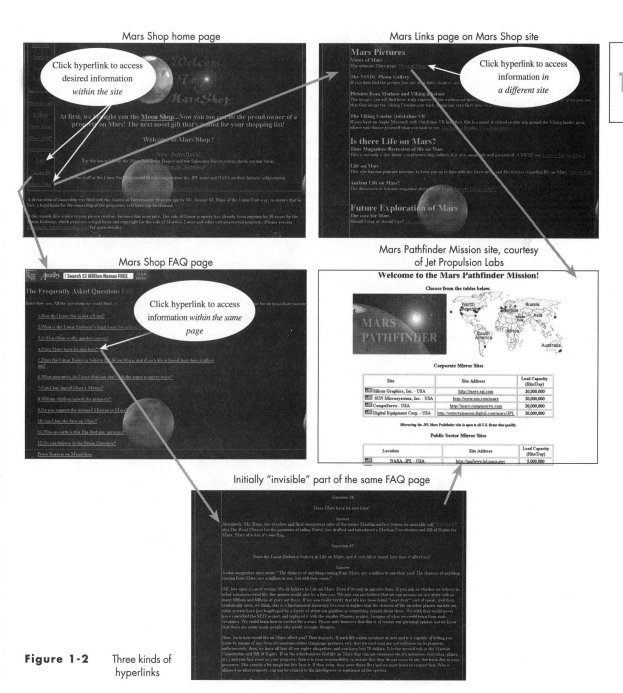

Figure 1-2 Three kinds of hyperlinks

Establishing a Web Presence

Since 1994 the Web has experienced astronomical growth, with organizations all over the globe advertising themselves and their wares to the world. An executive from one high-tech company, EDS (formerly Electronic Data Systems, Plano, Texas), estimates that the amount of information stored on the Web is growing by more than 20 terabytes (20,000,000,000,000 bytes, or characters) per week in about 650,000 new sites.[3] The number of people who access one or more pages of information has grown from 3 million worldwide to more than 40 million since 1994.[4] During the first half of the 1990s, companies created or updated their Web sites almost daily via the Internet, **intranets** (an Internet-like network that is internal to an organization), and **extranets** (an Internet-like network joining business organizations with common interests). Many companies have done well using the Web as a means for marketing and selling their products and services. In 1997, Cisco, Inc., a telecommunications company, realized $2 billion of its total $6 billion in sales over the Web.[5] Success stories like this have prompted many companies not currently on the Web to ask themselves, "What should we do about getting on the Web?" the assumption being that *something* must be done.

Ironically, the vehicle for all of this business and information exchange is a screen smaller than that of many televisions. Increasingly, people—customers, employees, and vendors—receive and act on information presented to them by means of video-type displays. A single screen—to which a person viewing a Web page devotes, on average, 6.8 seconds—often must carry the bulk of the company's message. If the initial presentation is emotionally and mentally pleasing, people will continue to read. If not, they will leave the Web site. So when a company wants to use the Web as a means of establishing a relationship with its marketplace, it must recognize the limitations as well as the strengths of this medium. Some companies, notably Amazon Books, have lost considerable money on their Web ventures.

Forming an ideal relationship requires imparting overall understandability, usability, and quality to the person visiting the site. This means coupling a skillful visual screen design with a clear, coherent message. Well-conceived text, attractive screen layouts, and stimulating graphic designs are fundamental to establishing a successful relationship between presenter and viewer. Without these elements, the presenter is likely to lose the viewer and may never establish a relationship.

Who is this "viewer"? **Viewers** are individuals who access and look at Web pages. There are basically two kinds of viewers: **surfers**—the millions of people who simply access pages and look at them—and **users**—people with a decided interest in the pages who acquire information from them and then make use of, or act on, that information.

Viewers are not a homogeneous group. They do not have a single perspective or single set of needs. Rather, they represent all possible perspectives, some of which become the object of design, not unlike

3. Web growth as of September 21, 1997. See http://www.mit.edu/people/mkgray/net/web-growth-summary.html

4. "A Census in Cyberspace," *Business Week,* May 5, 1997, 84.

5. J. Kerstettner, "Cisco Sites E-Commerce Success of Web Site," *PC Week Online,* May 5, 1997, at http://www8.zdnet.com/pcweek/news/0505/05ecis.html

the requirements to know your audience and speak to your reader in advertising, magazines, and all kinds of communications. *The main goal of a Web presentation is to fulfill users' information needs and wants.* Unfortunately, many pages in use today do not effectively fulfill users' needs for information and therefore will not convert surfers to users. For example, Figure 1-3 shows a Web page for the Blue Marble Advanced Communications Group. Notice that the page—which happens to be this Web site's **home page** (the first page the viewer sees on reaching the site)—gives no indication of the contents or purpose of the site and fails to convey any information about the company itself.

Figure 1-3   A home page with no clear intention

Another goal of a Web presentation is to visually please the user. Any surfing session will reveal the truly awesome at one end of the spectrum and the truly awful at the other. Some pages are bright and inviting; others are downright dull or garish, off-putting, even disgusting. A poorly designed page for an investment club is shown in Figure 1-4. It has no company identifier, no reference to the actual financial gain of the club, uneven placement of stock information, an ugly background, no information on the club itself, and no working mail link for "mail me."

If a home page is emotionally and cognitively pleasing, the viewer will go on to learn more about the Web site and its message. If not, the viewer leaves and may never return. In fact, if *any* Web page is not pleasing or useful or both, the viewer is likely to leave and unlikely to come back.

To summarize, seizing and keeping users' attention through visual aesthetics and relevant information is a major design challenge.

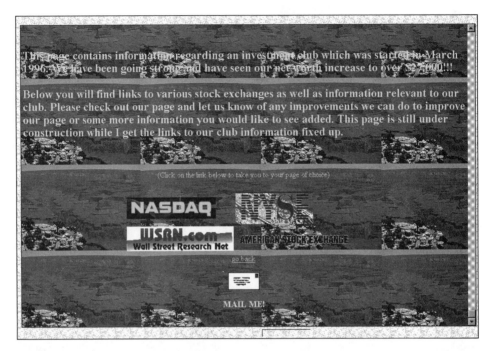

Figure 1-4 A badly designed Web page

The Design Challenge

Placing pages on the Web is deceptively simple. To develop a page, you simply create a word-processed document and embed the HTML codes to format the document for display on the Web. HTML is a fairly straightforward language, the basics of which can be learned in a few hours, as you will see when using the accompanying CD-ROM. This is the easy part of developing Web presentations.

It is a complex and formidable task to design a set of Web pages that effectively conveys information that can satisfy user needs and convert surfers to users. The site and its contents need to be:

- understandable
- interesting and valuable
- capable of converting surfers to users
- consistent and engaging
- a skillful integration of text, graphics, audio, video, and information extracted from databases
- easily navigated
- unified in look and feel

Three Overarching Criteria

The three essential criteria for designing a successful Web presentation are effectiveness, affectiveness, and navigational efficiency. **Effectiveness** is a rational criterion requiring that the presentation be complete, sensibly organized, and accurate in conveying the intended message. **Affectiveness** is an emotional criterion requiring that the presentation capture viewer attention by being interesting, stimulating, and enjoyable. **Navigational efficiency** refers to the ease with which users can locate the information they want. While effectiveness relates primarily to the mental—reasoning and thinking— states of users, affectiveness and navigational efficiency relate more to their emotional—artistic and feeling—states.

Successful Web presentations must satisfy all three of these criteria to some degree. Sometimes, however, one criterion can be satisfied only at the cost of giving up some aspects of another. For example, providing substantial amounts of information to achieve effectiveness may be achieved only by sacrificing some affectiveness and navigational efficiency. As shown in Figure C-1 (see color insert), trade-offs are often made to achieve the best overall result. Inexperienced designers often do not know how to make these trade-offs. As a result, users get lost in the pages or have a poor impression of the pages, both of which reflect unfavorably on the presenting organization.

The likelihood that a Web site will arrive at the optimum balance of effectiveness, affectiveness, and navigational efficiency can increase as the site goes through various generations of development. The likely changes in composition over successive generations of a Web presentation are diagrammed in Figure 1-5. Initial Web pages are often factual but dull, as is the case with the design of most industrial product manuals and university catalogues. That is, the text material may be *effective*, but it is not positively *affective*.

First-Generation Web Presentations

High effect typically results from formatting paper-based text as Web pages. We think of this as the **first generation** of a Web presentation. It reflects a print-based design (like an annual report) that does not translate well to the new media. *Content is important in Web presentations, but content alone will not "sell" pages.* More than likely, first-generation hyperlinks between pages are not developed on the basis of their potential relationships but for coincidental, text-based reasons.

Companies can track their Web site's usage statistics through server software that stores, for example, visitor identification, pages visited, and duration of visit for each page. A low number of page visits and visits of short duration are key indicators of first-generation design problems.

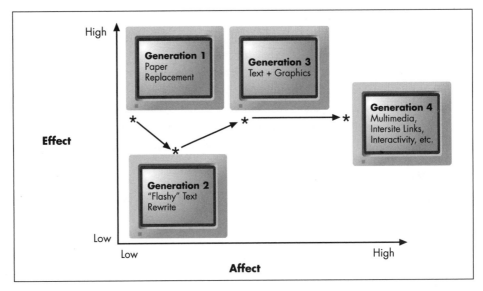

Figure 1-5   Typical evolution of Web presentations

Second-Generation Web Presentations

Once first-generation deficiencies are recognized, an effort is made to "spruce up" the presentation. This often results in a "flashy" design, but not much content. This **second-generation** Web presentation usually improves the site's affective properties because the text is redesigned and formatted according to guidelines for page layout. Usually graphics and decorative visuals are added. Some content may actually be removed during this iteration to provide more "white space" on each page. Such content removal may result in a drop in the overall effectiveness of the pages. Typically, second-generation Web sites have an excessive number of hyperlinks. This adds confusion and results in an overall drop in navigational efficiency. Viewer feedback through e-mail or comments pages on the site can identify problems with the second-generation solution.

Third-Generation Web Presentations

The **third generation** is usually the most difficult to produce successfully, because its goal is usually to avoid trade-offs between the three main criteria. It is designed consciously for presentation effect, affect, and efficiency. Thorough third-generation design requires a deeper understanding of:

- the intended user audience
- the purposes of the Web presentation
- the design demands, opportunities, and challenges of the media being used
- the information presented and the way it can be hyperlinked

Fourth-Generation Web Presentations and Beyond

Finally, effect, affect, and efficiency can be improved further in succeeding **generations** of the presentation as individual pieces of information are redesigned for multimedia, interactivity, or connection to other useful Web pages. Examples are "live" access to company information, forms or queries on order status that can be completed and sent to the company electronically, and so on. Linkages are rationalized further and redesigned to achieve more efficient, intuitive navigation and to increase affective links to other organizations' sites. Nonprofit associations (such as a chamber of commerce), independent organizations (such as Underwriter's Laboratories), and government organizations (such as the U.S. Department of Commerce) might provide additional pertinent information that increases a site's affect. Hyperlinks to other organizations, then, become desirable, no-cost sources of information for users.

The Understanding Business

Web pages have no value unless users understand and can act on the information they contain. Creating a Web presentation places you and your company in the "understanding" business. An **understanding business** provides information that is approachable, comprehensible, applicable, and useful. The primary goal of a company in developing a Web presentation is to promote understanding. Understanding is achieved when users use the pages and targeted surfers become users. Figure 1-6 shows the narrowing of a Web page audience from all people to a subset of surfers to a subset of targeted surfers to specific users. In the remainder of the discussion, we consciously use the term "user" because that is the primary audience of a Web presentation. The same discussion applies to targeted surfers—that is, the subset of the general audience to whom a presenter wants to appeal—but their needs might differ substantially from those of users.

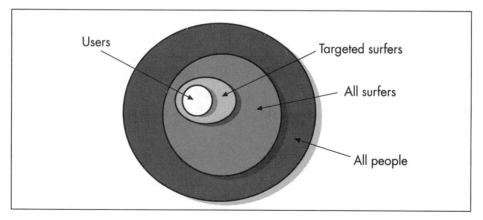

Figure 1-6   Users are a subset of surfers, who are a subset of all people

Thus, *the intent of a Web presentation is for a sponsoring organization, or presenter, and the user to reach a mutual understanding by means of their electronic connection.* When a user is finished viewing a Web site, the organization sponsoring it will have presented its intended message on its information, products, and services. At the same time, the user will have received that message, understood it, and matched it to his or her wants and needs. It is this electronic "meeting of the minds" that is essential to establishing a productive and lasting relationship in cyberspace. This simple, valuable point is illustrated in Figure 1-7.

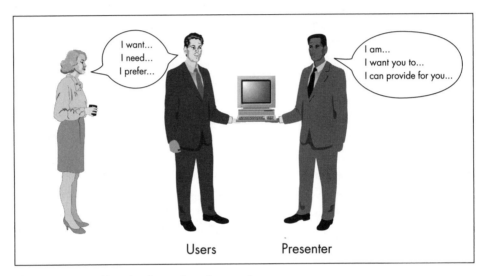

Figure 1-7 Mutual understanding of user and presenter

Two criteria must be met if mutual understanding is to be reached. First, the presenter must execute a design that reflects an accurate reading of the mental state of potential users, including their current knowledge, needs, preferences, and information-handling capabilities. Second, the user must have an accurate reading of the nature of the site, that is, understand why this particular information is being presented. **Mutual understanding** is achieved when a user's interpretation of a Web site matches the company's intentions for developing the site. Figure 1-8 illustrates the levels of mutual understanding possible between the company sponsoring the Web site and its users. Only high levels of organization and user understanding will have the desired outcome—a long-lasting relationship on the Web.

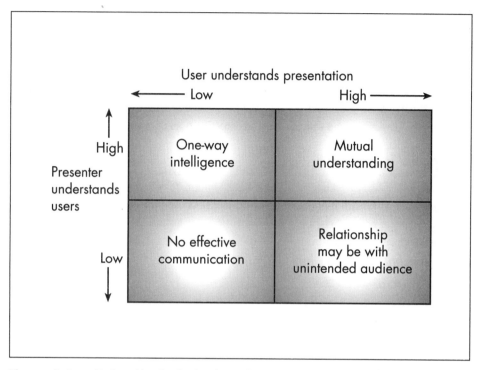

Figure 1-8   High and low levels of understanding

If neither criterion is satisfied, no effective communication takes place at all. If only the first requirement is satisfied, a one-way relationship results that at best is akin to market intelligence—that is, the presenter will gather more information on users, but users won't be persuaded (to buy goods, for instance), entertained, or informed. If only the second requirement is satisfied, a one-way relationship results in which the user is informed, indoctrinated, or trained in the company's message, but the company is not clear on the user's needs. In this instance, the users may be the appropriate audience and the sponsoring organization may not know who its customers are. Consequently, achievement of the goal of repeated contact cannot be expected.

On the Web, the crucial moment for reaching mutual understanding occurs when the user first accesses the presenting organization's home page. In a fleeting *seven seconds*, the user forms a partly mental, mostly emotional, impression of the company and of the information provided. If the impression is favorable, the user will continue to pay attention to the presentation, hyperlinking to additional pages. Ultimately, users leave the Web site when their task is complete or when their interest wanes. If the experience was successful, the user will have been appropriately entertained or found what he or she was looking for—that is, knowledge, merchandise, or services.

While users are navigating a site, they continually evaluate the progress they are making (or not making) toward their goals. Companies need to consider each user's experience as a journey, during which every page and its links are physical and emotional barriers that must be overcome to reach the desired destination. When a user visits a page, he or she makes progress toward mutual understanding and continues the electronic journey by hyperlinking to another Web page. If understanding is not reached or the content is not of interest, the user will not hyperlink to the next Web page, and the journey will end with the user disconnecting from the site.

Purpose in Design

Web presentations can have three basic purposes—to inform, to entertain, and to enable exchange. To **inform** is to provide the user with information that he or she wants and currently doesn't have. The user wants to obtain facts, learn something, or better understand something. Informational pages answer questions such as:

- What is it?
- Where is it?
- When does it take place?
- Who does it?
- How does it work?
- How much does it cost?
- How do I buy it?

GO to... http://www.thespot.com for an example of an entertainment page. The Spot is an ongoing story of a group of twenty-somethings that changes at least daily.

Good informational pages emphasize the completeness of the information provided. Informational pages require separation (decomposition) of the information into short, comprehensible **chunks**, also called **information objects**. Maps, tables, charts, graphs, simulations, animated illustrations, and audio and video clips are often used to supplement and complement text. Effectiveness criteria such as clarity, simplicity, directness, and reinforcement are most appropriate for use in designing pages to inform.

Pages designed to **entertain** provide amusement, relaxation, or diversion. Users of entertainment pages want to have fun, play a game, or engage in a new experience of some sort. Pages designed to entertain tend to emphasize whimsy, variety, surprise, and action. They often have bold color schemes and contain unpredictable events that change each time the user accesses the site. Affectiveness criteria are most appropriate for use in designing pages to entertain.

Pages that **enable exchange** allow users to perform some useful action—buy something, submit information, request information, answer questions, or otherwise interact with the site. Exchange pages tend to emphasize advertising, persuasion, and fast access. They usually include search facilities designed to help users find what they're looking for as quickly as possible, whether it's information, interactive order forms, e-mail addresses, registration forms, or toll-free phone numbers.

Threads Between Web Pages

Web presentations are designed to achieve a combination of these three basic purposes. Each basic purpose is represented by a set of pages held together by a thread of hyperlinks. A **thread** is like the trail of crumbs Hansel and Gretel left to find their way home through the forest. It is composed of the information on a series of Web pages, with hyperlinks identifying the location of the information and providing access to it. Each thread of a Web presentation has a primary purpose, such as exchange, but an organization's complete Web presentation should contain elements of all three purposes to maximize affect and effect.

Hybrid Web Pages

Three organizations with different primary purposes are The Dilbert Zone, the Dallas Federal Reserve, and Peapod grocery service, whose home pages are shown in Figure 1-9. The Federal Reserve's home page shows that its main goal is to provide useful, timely information about the Dallas bank, the Federal Reserve System, and the regional, national, and global economies. Elsewhere on its Web site the bank has a "send us email" option to meet a secondary goal of exchanging information.

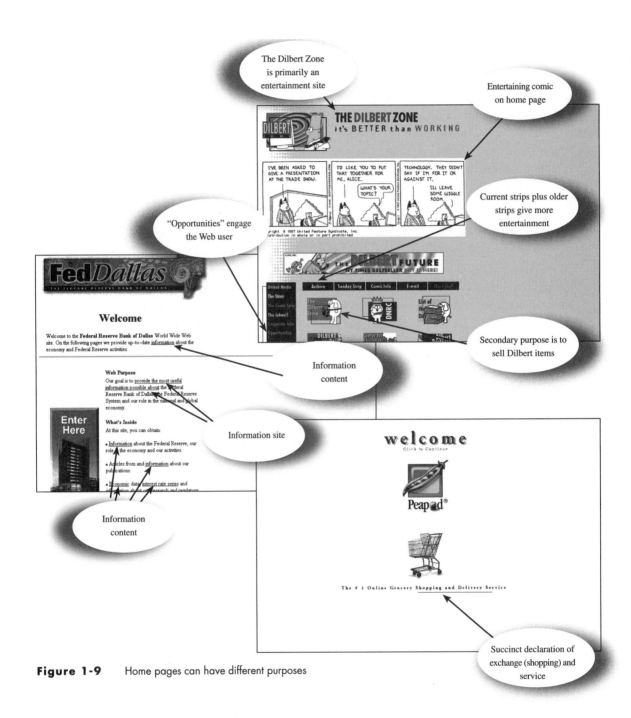

Figure 1-9   Home pages can have different purposes

In contrast, The Dilbert Zone pages stress entertainment, including games and contests. Because United Media wants to make purchasers out of users, the site also includes access to The Dilbert Store and to a list of licensed Dilbert vendors.

A third contrasting site is Peapod. The Peapod site is an exchange service used for on-line grocery shopping and delivery. It is designed to make shopping quick and easy.

Currently, many frameworks and methods for developing Web presentations are based on traditional approaches to management information systems development. But these traditional tools, techniques, and skills are inadequate for Web presentation development. This is because they don't address the type of design or media considerations necessitated by the Web. The methodology presented in this text addresses specific Web presentation development needs. The techniques are scalable and can be used to develop a Web site of any size at any location (Internet, intranet, or extranet).

The crucial first step in Web presentation design, then, is to determine the purpose or purposes for offering the information. Subsequently these purposes must be matched to those of users. This can turn into a "which came first, the chicken or the egg?" sort of problem. Whose concerns should be considered first? The Web site's user or its sponsor? In fact, the interests of both should be defined simultaneously and be continually reevaluated and intertwined throughout Web site development, design, and redesign.

Chapter 2 discusses the participants involved in developing Web presentations. Participants should aim to develop user-centered, user-valued designs. To achieve this goal, however, the person actually designing the presentation— the designer—must work closely with others in their organization. We examine these other roles first. While reading the next chapter, keep in mind that the participants described are **ideal types**, that is, a precise and distinct version of a role. In fact, the roles may be played by one, two, or many people, depending on the organization and its Web strategy.

 W e b   D e s i g n   i n   t h e   R e a l   W o r l d

Best Personalized Books

Recall that Best Personalized Books develops and sells software for producing custom personalized books. The company uses a licensing arrangement to sell its books. A **licensee** is someone who purchases the software for a specific purpose, in this case, to create personalized books using the Best process. The license allows software upgrade purchases and licensee variations on products to be sold.

Best sells the software, paper stock, and book covers as part of the licensing arrangement. Licensees obtain the personalizing information for each book, such as a child's name, relatives' names, pets' names, and so on. Using the software, the licensee accesses a **template**, or skeleton, of the story and enters the new information to customize the specific book, as shown in Figure 1-10. Once the customized information has been inserted into the text on disk, the entire story is printed out on the paper stock provided by Best, and the book is bound. The books can be sold in a variety of ways, including mail order, in person (such as at school book fairs), over the Web, or through brochures dropped off at local businesses for customer use.

When Best's owners, Jack and Wendy Kalisher, began to consider the Web site development project, they were careful to review the process of design, analysis, and implementation. Before the process could begin, however, the project participants and their respective roles needed to be established. This is the subject of Chapter 2.

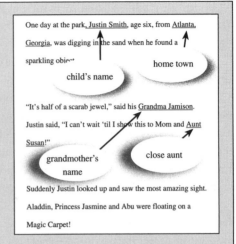

One day at the park, Justin Smith, age six, from Atlanta, Georgia, was digging in the sand when he found a sparkling object

child's name

home town

"It's half of a scarab jewel," said his Grandma Jamison. Justin said, "I can't wait 'til I show this to Mom and Aunt Susan!"

grandmother's name

close aunt

Suddenly Justin looked up and saw the most amazing sight. Aladdin, Princess Jasmine and Abu were floating on a Magic Carpet!

Figure 1-10
Sample text from a Best book

Summary

The World Wide Web is becoming the primary vehicle for electronic business. Development of Web presentations that foster appropriate use is a challenge for companies seeking to operate in the cyber world of commerce. The challenge is to define appropriate user groups and decide how best to provide the services and information they desire. Designing Web presentations requires a combination of design goals for effectiveness, or completeness and accuracy; affectiveness, or emotional appeal; and navigational efficiency, or the required breadth of intuitively designed linkages.

The intent of a Web presentation is for the presenting organization and the Web user to reach a **mutual understanding** through the Web connection. This implies that the presenting organization must understand both who the users are and what they need and want from the Web connection. Users come to mutual understanding when the Web presentation design provides an accurate understanding of the presenter's intentions and capabilities.

The three main purposes of a Web presentation are to **inform**, to **entertain**, or to **enable some exchange** (for instance, a sale). The challenge for those creating Web presentations is to blend these purposes in an effective, affective, and navigationally efficient manner to reach mutual understanding between the user and the organization. The goals and trade-offs of these challenges are the subject of this text.

R e v i e w   Q u e s t i o n s

1. What is the difference between a surfer and a user? Why is this difference important?

2. What does it mean to say that a Web presenter has reached a state of mutual understanding with a Web user?

3. What is a URL? What do each of its components stand for?

4. What is the difference between the criterion of effectiveness and the criterion of affectiveness? What is the importance of each in contributing to a Web site's success?

5. What is meant by navigational efficiency? How does it relate to the concept of a thread?

6. What are the three primary purposes of Web presentations? How do the primary purposes relate to the design criteria of effectiveness, affectiveness, and navigational efficiency?

7. What characteristics distinguish a first generation Web presentation from second and third generations?

8. Why must designers make trade-offs between effectiveness, affectiveness, and navigational efficiency?

9. What is the importance of making the first, or home, page of a Web site easy to digest? How long does the average surfer look at a page?

10. What does HTTP mean, and how does it relate to the Internet?

P r o j e c t s

In this section of each chapter, two kinds of projects are presented. The first group will be surfing exercises with questions that relate to the chapter material, or general projects. For students without access to the Internet, Web pages are stored on the CD-ROM that accompanies the text to do these exercises. The second are ongoing projects. In one ongoing project, to be completed over the course of the semester, you work with a local professor, department, or organization to plan, design, and develop a Web site, progressing through each of the phases presented in this book. This chapter also presents another hands-on activity, helping you customize a Web-based resume with HTML.

1. Surf the Web (or CD-ROM) for a set of pages that interest you. What purpose do you think the presenting company had in mind? Who do you think are the pages' intended users? How would surfers respond to this page? In your judgment, is mutual understanding achieved between company and user? How well does the page meet the criteria of effectiveness, affectiveness, and navigational efficiency?

2. Find a second set of Web pages offered by an organization similar to or competing with the organization from question 1. Answer the same questions. Compare the two sets of pages.

3. Surf through as many pages as you can. Identify the set of pages that best satisfies the following objectives: informative, entertaining, engaging in exchange, easily navigated, visually pleasing, well-organized information effect. In the browser, use the "add bookmark" or "add favorites" function to store the URL for future reference.

C a s e   P r o j e c t

1. Select an organization or department or some topic, product, or service of your own to make available on the Web. Describe the project briefly. What are the purposes of making the information available? Who will be the users? How important are the criteria of effectiveness, affectiveness, and navigational efficiency for making this project a success?

2. On the CD-ROM, complete the assignment at the end of Chapter 1 to develop a Web-based resume.

F u r t h e r   R e a d i n g

- Anderson, Christopher. "In Search of the Perfect Market." *The Economist*, May 10, 1997, 72-79.
- Bush, Vannevar. "As We May Think." *The Atlantic Monthly*, July 1945, 101-108.
- "A Census in Cyberspace." *Business Week*, May 5, 1997, 84-85.
- Kerstettner, Jim. "Cisco Sites E-Commerce Success of Web Site," *PC Week Online*, May 5, 1997, at http://www8.zdnet.com/pcweek/news/0505/05ecis.html
- Nelson, Theodor H. *Literary Machines* (Swarthmore, Pa.: Mindful Publications, 1981). Quoted in George P. Landrow, *Hypertext: The Convergence of Contemporary Critical Theory and Technology* (Baltimore, Md.: Johns Hopkins University Press, 1992).
- "Special Report on Internet Communities." *Business Week*, May 5, 1997, 64-83.

2

The Roles of Web Creators and the Reactions of Users

In This Chapter You Will Learn To:

- Describe the roles of those people involved in developing a Web presentation—presenter, information steward, and designer
- Explain the importance of user-centered Web design
- Explain the importance of information stewards' control and approval of the design and content of the Web presentation
- Describe the skills required of the Web designer—information elicitation, semantic understanding, information analysis, design, and technical skills
- Describe the basic types of user reaction to Web presentations and their significance to presentation design

Web Design in the Real World

Best Personalized Books

The first issue in developing the Web site for Best Personalized Books was to determine who would participate. Web projects involve many different people, playing several different roles. In the case of Best, Sue Conger (author of this book) approached Jack and Wendy—her neighbors—to see if they'd be interested in developing a Web site for their company. Sue and coauthor Dick Mason would provide their services as Web development specialists free of charge, in

exchange for Jack and Wendy's willingness to have their experience documented in this book. (*Note to reader:* This arrangement is similar to that which you might offer prospective participants in your Web design project. Keep in mind that the project should be finite since it must be completed in several weeks. Also, try to find clients who are flexible in working around your class deadlines.) Once Jack and Wendy agreed, they sat down with Sue and Dick to begin planning for the project.

Understanding the Roles of Web Creators

The roles of individuals in a company developing a Web site include presenters, information stewards, and designers. These roles can be performed by a single individual, several people, or a large group of people. Each of these roles and their corresponding tasks in the process—which are reviewed briefly in Figure 2-1—are crucial to developing a Web site that presents the organization in the desired manner. If the team is established without all of these roles being filled, the Web presentation may fail, perhaps by presenting inappropriate information or by presenting the organization in an unfavorable way.

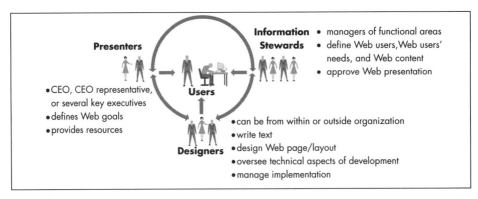

Presenters
- CEO, CEO representative, or several key executives
- defines Web goals
- provides resources

Users

Information Stewards
- managers of functional areas
- define Web users, Web users' needs, and Web content
- approve Web presentation

Designers
- can be from within or outside organization
- write text
- design Web page/layout
- oversee technical aspects of development
- manage implementation

Figure 2-1　A Web development team includes several levels of organizational managers—all working together to engage users

The Presenter: The Ultimate Decision Maker

Presenters are the people representing a corporation or organization who are responsible for deciding the scope of the Web application and for allocating resources to it. They have ultimate decision-making authority over the project. Their purposes, goals, and objectives govern Web application development activities.

The presenter may be a single individual, but more often an entire organization and its key executives take on the role of presenter. Executives in each functional area of the business are presenters of their area of responsibility. This group decides on the overall strategy that determines what information to present on the Web, what information not to present, and what resources will be needed in terms of personnel and funding. Presenters should decide what information should be shared not only with current customers and the like, but also with the rest of the world. Since these decisions often involve making trade-offs, they can—and often should—be made by the highest level of management, that is, the CEO or his or her representative.

Presenters may have a lot at stake when they make these decisions. The Web presentation can be viewed by users located anywhere in the world. If the wrong information is presented, it is disseminated to a large audience, and the damage to the presenting company can be significant. The differences between large and small organizations can be virtually invisible to Web users, depending on the resources the organization is willing to allocate to its Web site. The larger the organization, the more it has to lose if its Web application does not attract users. A well-established company, big or small, can do damage to its image and lose prestige and goodwill if its Web application is poorly designed. The cost to the large company may be especially high because the likelihood of its failure being noticed and commented on by the press is far greater. When that happens, what might have been a small problem becomes a disaster.

In addition to deciding what information to present on the Web, the presenter also has to determine the Web presentation's level of interactivity with the company's current internal information systems (IS), such as inventory management. This decision can have far-reaching consequences for internal organizational IS development. It should be made by executives and managers at a level of authority that encompasses all of the affected functional areas. Decisions of this kind may have material effects that extend far beyond that of Web page design. For instance, both applications and Web servers need different levels of security when corporate information is being presented on the Web. Planning and implementing such security can take months.

The Information Steward: Keeper of Information

A steward is a person who manages someone else's property, finances, or affairs. Information stewards manage someone else's—usually their employer's—information, some of which will be used in the Web presentation. Information stewards can be, but are not necessarily, the same people as the presenters (although, as just mentioned, they frequently work for the presenters' organization). They may or may not participate in the design process, but as guardians of vital company or organizational information, their cooperation and approval are absolutely necessary to the development of a Web site.

Information stewards are often identified by their role in the presenting organization. For example, in a typical presenting organization, the information stewards might include the manager of public relations, the manager of customer service, the manager of manufacturing, the manager of marketing, and so on. Many stewards might be on the Web development team. The group of stewards can expand to include all people who, by their organizational position, have custody of, responsibility for, or influence over information targeted for Web presentation.

Information stewards' primary responsibility is to determine *who* Web users are, and then consequently their wants and needs. For example, the public relations manager best understands the type of information wanted by members of the general public. Similarly, the customer service manager will most likely understand customer needs. Once the users and their wants and needs are defined, stewards need to determine the threads, or the natural progressions, that run through the information, so that different types of information can be linked together. Finally, stewards participate in testing the information and the threads running through it to make sure they match the needs of one or more user groups.

Web presentations must communicate well with a vast audience—the approximately 60 million people who currently connect to the Internet. Determining the information, products, and services to be presented on the Web requires determining the full range of desired viewers, including users who will be served and surfers who will not. Information stewards possess the expertise and knowledge necessary to define these viewers. Just as important, information stewards have the task of authorizing the form and manner in which information is presented. The actual *creation* of the Web presentation that uses this information is the responsibility of the designer.

The Designer: Technical Guru, Wordsmith, Media Designer

Web presentation design has been called an "emerging 21st century professional occupation addressing the needs of the age focused upon clarity, human understanding, and the science of the organization of information."[1] The designer is responsible for developing a Web application, beginning with information and materials collection and ending with a fully operational application. Designers must create a Web presentation that achieves mutual understanding between presenters and users, while meeting the demands of information stewards. To do this well, they must be able to generate a variety of design alternatives and therefore be familiar with many different approaches to Web page composition.

Designers must be able to estimate how well each alternative satisfies the purposes of the users, presenters, and stewards. Herein lies one difficulty for designers. Designers must satisfy both the presenters and the users of Web pages. Because the users are the ultimate "clients" of the Web site, their wants and needs must be satisfied. But the presenters are also a "client"—of the designer. The project must also satisfy their interests. To ensure that the appropriate resources are allocated to the project, the designer must address the presenters' interests and concerns. This dual responsibility

1. Richard Saul Wurman, *Information Architecture* (Zurich: Graphics Press, 1996).

creates a tension for the designer between presenter and user—satisfying one group might mean not satisfying the other. Consequently, designers and presenters must make difficult "trade-off" decisions to balance presenter demands and user requirements.

Finally, designers must be able to communicate to others—programmers, graphic artists, writers, managers, and perhaps the designers who will maintain the Web site—how their thoughts are to be converted into action so that the application meets the established objectives.

In Web design, the affective, effective, and efficiency components are ultimately under the control of the information steward, even though the design work is executed by a designer. While writing clear, concise, and understandable text is a required skill for the design team, the final expression of the text should be approved by the relevant information steward(s). Many information stewards, however, believe they have precious little time to devote to "wordsmithing" Web pages. As a result, most of this task often falls to the designer, with (it is hoped) the stewards' approval. This can be a satisfying situation, provided the designer has good grammatical skills, and can verify and update the accuracy and completeness of the information.

Web designer skills differ from those of a designer of traditional internal IS applications. Traditional application design requires the designer to understand the user domain (how the application will be used), the application development domain (work and data processes to be automated), and the technology domain (the actual automation via program code, databases, and the like). The task of traditional application development, generally speaking, is to translate requirements from the user domain to the application development domain and then again to the technological domain.

A significantly expanded skill set is required for Web presentation design and any graphical interface design. The expanded skill set for designers working on Web presentations is outlined in Figure 2-2. Specifically, Web designers require additional semantic, design, and technical skills.

- Understanding of information, semantics
- Ability to translate information into a structure
- Ability to translate structure into text and pages
- Artistic sensibility that translates into capacity for visualization, color sense, page layout, multimedia selection and use
- Capacity for language selection and use
- Facility with multimedia technology, selection, item creation techniques, implementation, web storage
- Facility with database technologies, Web access, security

Figure 2-2   Knowledge and skills needed by Web presentation designers

Semantic skills refer to understanding the meaning behind verbal and written information. Web designers study the information content and its mode of expression. Semantic skills are needed to execute several phases of Web application development, including:

- specifying information domains (an information domain defines the scope of interest, what is within or not within the bounds of the topic of interest, in this case a Web presentation)
- defining the content of each information domain in detail with the appropriate information stewards
- translating information domains into a set of information objects
- mapping the relationships between information objects

These semantic skills, then, include a mixture of verbal abilities. The designer needs to understand the meaning of the words and to interpret the importance of variations on the meanings for the company. He or she also needs to translate the company's information into coherent text, and to link ideas from multiple departments into a coherent interpretation of the organization and its information.

Visual skills also are required of Web designers. At a minimum, designers need knowledge of multimedia tools and techniques, multimedia selection, graphic design, page layout, and multimedia design capabilities.

Visual skills include the ability to be mindful of user and technical limitations. Screen display must be designed to bring together two very powerful information-processing capabilities: a telecommunications-capable computer and the human mind. The designer's goal is to communicate with the user via an effective, affective, and efficient Web presentation delivered through a display screen. The display screen constrains space. Even though the average screen supports roughly 36,000 characters of information at a time, most of it should be left unused so as to minimize the amount of time the user will spend trying to understand the information. From 40 to 60 percent of any given Web page should be white space (that is, empty of text). As mentioned earlier, the average time a surfer views a Web page is under seven seconds.

Additional technical skills are also required to translate page and multimedia designs into the digital realm. Because they are specific to the particular technology, these skills can be quite specialized and varied. Each technology serves a limited number of media and has its own specific knowledge and skill requirements. A single Web page might include audio recording and playback objects developed using RealAudio, for example. RealAudio requires knowledge of treble tones, bass tones, and midtones; recording technologies (tools that digitize sound); script writing; recording (narration, sound effects, etc.); electronic mastering and editing; and storage of audio objects for Web use. Conversely, the same Web page might include functions for users, such as order entry, and would be developed in a programming language such as Java or ActiveX. The designer's proficiency in programming languages must include not only knowledge of the language and the ability to break down a problem into solvable sections, but also knowledge of specialized code for Web access, data manipulation, Web and local security, and Web storage techniques.

Sometimes, the designer gets information in a format that is not usable on the Web and so must reformat the information so that it can be used on the Web. Security and firewalls must also be developed to guard against unwanted intrusions (the result of corporate espionage or hacker break-ins, for example). Actual development of these safeguards may be done by the designer or by internal IS people. In any case, the designer must be aware of the need for the safeguards and be able to convey the requirements.

Given the varied and demanding nature of the complement of skills required, Web page design is often best done by teams. All the needed skills are rarely found in a single person, and designers must constantly upgrade their knowledge as new technologies become available.

Designers must become skillful in working with presenters, stewards, content experts, writers, editors, researchers, graphics artists, animators, video professionals, and interface designers and programmers. The ability to work with presenters and stewards is required of all Web designers, no matter what technology is being used. The other specialists will join the Web development team only when the designers do not have those skills themselves, or when the presentation has so much information that many people are required to implement it in a reasonable amount of time. Being able to judge these parties' contributions and effectively coordinate activities are other characteristics of a good designer.

Overall, designer skills tend to be split between those dealing with the presentation team and the information and those dealing with technology. When the designer is part of a team of designers, then coordination, team-building, and project management skills are also necessary.

So far, the discussion of roles in the presentation has focused on participants in a single organization developing a Web presentation useful to users. In the next section, we change the focus to *users* of the Web application, distinguishing between surfers and users.

Understanding Users

Users do not visit a Web site without some preconceived ideas. They have a model of the world in their heads, a **mental map**, built on the basis of their culture and experience, which provides structure for their thoughts and actions. Most users are looking for information that fits with, or can be absorbed readily into, their existing worldview. That means that in designing a Web site it's important to use an organizational scheme that matches users' mental maps as closely as possible; information must be presented in such a way that it makes intuitive sense to the user.

Consider a company intranet that presents policies and procedures for employees. Employees go to the intranet when they need to know about job conduct policies, leave policies for vacation, illness, and emergencies, and the like. When they get there, they will expect to find the information organized into some sort of menu that matches their intuition and expectations—as shown in the left-hand column in Figure 2-3. They will not expect (or probably much like) a randomly assorted list—as shown in the right-hand column of the figure. In the intuitively organized list, like topics are grouped, and the information provided moves from general to specific. In the randomly organized list, such topics as the company's stock price history are side by side with information on health benefits—surely not a helpful association. If a Web site's set of menus does not reflect an intuitive understanding of the user's mental map, the presentation will not be used. Matching Web presentation design to a user's mental map is necessary, and it means matching the information organization, page layout, threads for navigation—the whole presentation design. This intuitive knowledge will promote the desired state of mutual understanding described in Chapter 1.

Intuitive Information Organization	Random Information Organization

•Personnel policies
 -Health care
   -Medical insurance
   -Sick leave policies
 -Vacation
 -Other leaves of absence
•Customer sales tracking
•Stock
 -Price
 -History
	•Health care policies
	•Stock price
	•Vacation and other leaves
	•Customer sales tracking
	•Sick leave policies
	•Medical insurance
	•Stock history
	•Other leaves of absence

Figure 2-3   Intuitive information relationships vs. random information organization

Some users are looking for information that will change, adapt, or adjust their models of the world and provide a new context in which to obtain new information. And this is often the intention of presenters—to share their values with users and bring users around to their point of view. Presentations designed to change their users' opinions must include powerful graphical and persuasion techniques. For instance, a site for an upcoming movie shows clips of the film's most exciting scenes, to persuade viewers to see the film.

User Reactions to Web Presentations

When viewing a Web presentation, a person's senses—seeing, hearing, and to a lesser extent touching—are selective. For a Web presentation to be successful, it must first attract the user's attention. This attention—the concentration of the user's mental powers on the Web pages—is the chief asset the user brings to a session of Web browsing. Most users are willing to devote only a small amount of attention to each Web page in a presentation, but they will continue to view those pages if what they see is sufficiently rewarding. A particular page may be selected for continued viewing because it stands out from the rest or because it responds to the user's needs.

Once the presentation has gained the user's attention, the information in it is perceived. Technically speaking, perception is the neurological process by which recognition and interpretation take place. It involves taking the raw, unorganized stimuli

GO to...

http//www.amnesty.org for an example of Amnesty International's Web presentation, which is designed to persuade users to get involved in resolving social injustices around the world. It seeks to persuade users to take the company's perspective on the issue presented.

experienced by the senses and organizing them into the context of previous experience. During perception, a user's memory works in conjunction with the sensory stimuli to produce images and thoughts. What a user perceives first are edges, shapes, relationships, lights, shadows, and a sense of the whole. This is why typography, layout, and graphic design play such a crucial role in Web page design: these are the elements that the user first perceives. As the mind perceives the edges, shapes, and so on, it interprets them as elements with meaning.

Users do two things with the images and thoughts that form in their minds: they feel them, reacting to them artistically and emotionally, and they think about them. Feelings can involve a full range of *emotional* responses—for example, joy, excitement, serenity, anger, or revulsion. Thinking includes a full range of *mental* processes—including selection, combination, separation, correction, completion, synthesis, abstraction, simplification, and problem solving. User behavior ultimately results from these feeling and thinking processes. A Web presentation must motivate the user to engage in these processes so that he or she is moved to take action.

Remember, different users view a Web presentation with different goals in mind. A Web presentation needs to offer different kinds of messages to accommodate different users.

Because the user is continuously evaluating the progress being made toward his or her goal, each facet of the Web presentation must engage the user's cognitive processes (recognizing, interpreting, thinking, etc.). At the same time, a user's capacity to cope with complexity and volumes of information is limited. According to psychologists, people are able to deal with only five to nine concepts at one time or, as this capacity is often referred to, the magical 7 ± 2. This human limitation means that the entire mass of material in a Web presentation must be broken down into modules or information units, each of which is brief, concise, and singular, that is, containing a single fact, thought, or idea. These units are organized into a tree structure, as shown in Figure 2-4, generally with about five to nine units at each level. This process of breaking down information is known as **chunking.**

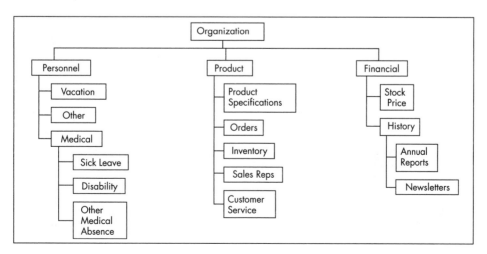

Figure 2-4   Typical tree-structure diagram Web site

Users often experience information anxiety when using the Web. **Information anxiety** is an uncomfortable feeling of dread that occurs when a person feels unable to understand a situation. In the case of the Web, "there are several general situations likely to induce information anxiety: Not understanding information; feeling overwhelmed by the amount of information to be understood; not knowing if certain information exists; not knowing where to find information; and, perhaps the most frustrating, knowing exactly where to find the information, but not having the key to access it."[2]

The effectiveness of Web presentations in providing concise, easily understood, complete, and accurate information soothes information anxiety and helps turn it into information proficiency. **Information proficiency** is the opposite of information anxiety, that is, it is a feeling of competence and complete understanding. Affectiveness—in being emotionally consistent throughout a site, and effectiveness—in matching the user's mental map—also increases the likelihood that a user will gain information proficiency. Finally, navigational efficiency makes it easier for the user to determine what actions are available, how those actions relate to the pages, and how to take them. The more that interpage navigation is made intuitive, natural, and easy to use, the more proficient and less anxious the user will be.

The guidelines and principles of design discussed in the following chapters are based on this understanding of users and their psychology. User attributes should be defined and considered carefully by designers. However, in the end designers must always make trade-offs as they attempt to satisfy different user groups while meeting the presenter's goals.

Web Design in the Real World

Best Personalized Books

For Best Personalized Books, the presenters were Jack and Wendy Kalisher, the owners of the company. They were also represented by Mike Heischman—the information systems manager—and Sandra Jones—Jack's staff assistant—who acted as occasional information stewards. Most of the time, Wendy acted as the information steward and Jack acted as the presenter. They were both involved in all aspects of the design and development. The principal designers for the project were Sue Conger and Dick Mason.

Jack and Wendy's motivations for developing the Web presentation were as follows:

1. A competitor's licensee had recently developed a Web site to sell books. To remain competitive, the company needed to move its operations onto the Web.

2. Jack believed that on-line support for customer and licensee inquiries and orders would increase Best's penetration of global markets.

2. Richard Saul Wurman, *Information Anxiety* (New York: Bantam Books, 1989), 44.

3. The Web site was expected to help manage their customer service demand, which currently required several toll-free phone lines and was growing faster than anticipated.

The group—Jack, Wendy, Sue, and Dick—met several times to discuss the project. At the initial meeting, Jack described the company background and gave a tour of their facility. This helped Sue to develop an understanding of the company and its products and services.

An overall approach to the Web presentation was discussed, but no major decisions were made except to agree that every attempt would be made to include as much of Best's existing print media text and graphics as possible. Most of this material was in the form of company brochures and handouts, similar to the one shown in Figure 2-5. This would provide continuity between print and Web media, lower costs, and reduce the time it would take to develop customized Web graphics and content.

Possible user groups were discussed. Sue proposed the following: individual book purchasers, library book purchasers, potential licensees, and current licensees. For individual purchasers, the idea was to sell books directly to the consumers who wanted to order on the Web. Since only individuals currently bought Best books, it made sense to provide purchasing opportunities to this group.

Libraries were the second proposed class of users. A link for libraries would open a new market. Sue's thinking was that libraries might be expected to buy in bulk,

Figure 2-5
Best Personalized Books brochure

personalizing many names to add appeal to young library users.

Potential licensees—the third class of users—could be given the information that would enable them, should they decide to become a licensee, to print a licensing agreement and order inventory and software directly from the Web. This capability was expected to cut down on the phone customer support and also save time for highly-motivated new licensees.

Finally, current licensees would have more information available to them than the other user classes via protected password access. Through this secured facility, they would be able to order supplies and inventory directly. This capability would also reduce the strain on the customer support phone lines.

The ideas for soliciting libraries and individual sales were shot down immediately. Jack made it clear that they did not sell direct and that libraries were not in their market concept—only licensees were. Jack explained that the direct licensing business is successful specifically because after an individual buys the license, Best is under no obligation other than to respond to the individual's questions and purchase requests. Best does not actually *sell* the books—they sell the materials to make books and license software to produce them. The concept of licensing is similar to franchising, although subject to different regulations and taxes.

Direct selling to individual buyers was vetoed for the same reason. Jack felt that individual sales would be perceived as a competitive move by Best against its licensees; he had no desire to sell direct and did not want to compete with his licensees, either. He did think that some information for potential licensees should be available.

Wendy reviewed the current process of obtaining a license since she was uncomfortable with a Web-only sale of licenses, too. Currently, a potential licensee could call the company, talk to a marketing representative, and purchase a license. Or they might first get literature and then go through this process. Wendy's concern was that with no phone qualification of potential licensees, Best could not ensure a licensee's level of motivation or understanding of the product, licensee obligations, and the costs involved.

Jack was also concerned about providing all licensing information on the Web; he was in favor of providing the toll-free number for further qualification.

Wendy's and Jack's concerns were too important to ignore and did not seem to have a simple resolution. The decision at the time was to provide potential licensees with information only. Sue suggested they try to think of Web solutions that met their concerns and still provided for the potential licensee user group. She felt this was important because experience had shown that user groups who feel their needs are not met become vocal critics of the site and, by extension, the company.

Next, the discussion turned to current licensees. The presentation content for current licensees was defined to include marketing, sales support, hot news, a company newsletter, and ordering information. Licensees could only access this information using a password. Another meeting was scheduled to continue the discussion and reach firm decisions about the user groups and their wants and needs.

The purposes of the Web pages that developed at these meetings were as follows:

1. The Web pages would provide non-licensee surfers with information about the company, which, it was hoped, would motivate them to call a toll-free number for more information and thereby convert them into users.

2. The site would provide current licensees with protected marketing information and product-ordering capability.

S   u   m   m   a   r   y

A Web presentation is designed to inform, entertain, or encourage users to engage in some exchange activity. It should also convert targeted groups of Web surfers into users.

There are three organizational roles that are crucial to developing a Web presentation: presenter, information steward, and designer. These roles may be played by one, several, or a group of highly specialized individuals. The individuals are all representatives of the presenting organization, whether they are its employees or hired external consultants. Ideally, presenters and stewards are from within the organization, while designers can be from within or outside the organization.

Presenters are key senior managers who are responsible for a Web presentation's overall strategy, information content, resource allocation, and extent of integration with other organizational advertising. Because company size, age, and ability to develop a quality product or service is invisible on the Web, corporate image is an important component of the deliberations leading to strategic Web decisions.

The information stewards are responsible for defining sources of information, users, user needs and wants, and threads that tie different types of information together. Ideally, stewards are full participants throughout the preparation and design stages of Web presentation development. If not full participants, at a minimum they approve all work and provide management guidance for their portion of the Web presentation. Each steward is fully responsible for final wording of text, final selection of media, and the overall look and feel of their portion of the presentation. The information stewards on the development team are fully responsible for the Web presentation contents.

Designers have the role of gathering all potential information for the Web presentation, analyzing and decomposing it, defining the overall structure of the Web presentation, developing alternatives, proposing media and technologies, and implementing all of the required design technologies. Because of these duties, the skill set of designers for Web presentations is broad, including graphical, visualization, semantic, technical, implementation, security, and interpersonal skills.

These roles—presenter, information steward, and designer—can rarely be filled by a single person. So, in addition to all of the above skills, interpersonal skills for coordination, performance evaluation, and project management are required.

An understanding of user reactions—basically, thinking and feeling—to Web presentations is crucial to a successful development effort. A Web presentation must:

- capture and maintain the user's attention within seven seconds
- stimulate the desired behavior by matching the user's mental maps from initial attention through perception, thinking, feeling and, eventually, action
- satisfy one or more of the user's needs

To satisfy these needs, conscious definition of each class of user and its specific needs and desires is required.

R e v i e w   Q u e s t i o n s

1. How does an information steward differ from a presenter? Why is the distinction important?

2. What skills are required for Web presentation designers?

3. What is an information domain? Why is it important that it be clearly defined early in a Web development project?

4. How does an information domain relate to the criteria of effectiveness, affectiveness, and navigational efficiency?

5. Which designer skills are you most likely to improve by taking this course? By taking a computer programming course? By taking a graphical design course? What other courses or experiences would help you develop the different types of designer skills?

6. Comment on the statement, "The medium is the message." (Marshall McLuhan, 1950s commentator on new media). How does this idea relate to Web presentations? Do you agree with this statement? Why or why not?

P r o j e c t s

1. Surf the Web for pages offered by Fortune 500 organizations. Choose one set of pages you think is well done and another you think is ineffective. Try to define the presenter for each. Define the site sponsor's view of the users, type of threads needed, and goals for the Web application. To what extent do you think these decisions were a conscious part of the design? To what extent do you think the decisions affected the quality of the application?

2. Surf the Web and find a page that appeals to you. Try to consciously define your emotional and intellectual reactions to the page. Describe the layout and content and how your eyes follow the design to move to various page elements. Try to define aspects of the design that capture and focus your attention. How do you make sense of the page content from the design elements? What are the emotional or aesthetic responses you feel toward the design? What actions are inspired by observing and experiencing the design? Try to define the extent of information resolution between you and the page presenter. What could be done to improve the information resolution? Conversely, what design elements detract from information resolution?

3. Take the assignment in #2 above and locate a Web page that you do not like. Do the same analysis.

C a s e   P r o j e c t

 1. For the company for which you are developing a Web presentation, identify the key organizational role players (presenters, information stewards, and designers) in the organization.

 2. Schedule a brief interview with the presenter(s) to identify their goals for the Web presentation, resources to be allocated, commitment to the Web presentation, and major decisions for which you will need their approval. For each information steward, define the information he/she controls. Define each person's commitment to providing that information. To what degree will they participate in the collection and review of this information (that is, what tasks are they willing to complete, and what tasks are they only willing to approve)? Define what you must do to complete the job without the steward, if necessary.

 3. Working with the presenters and stewards, be as specific as possible in identifying the users they anticipate. Try to place yourself in the head and mind of a typical viewer (a process called "empathy"). Use your own experience surfing the Web to define contents and a design that would convert you into a user of this intended site. Develop assumptions about classes of users and their information needs and potential uses. Define how to capture viewer attention.

 4. Describe the design challenge facing you in completing your project. Make an inventory of your current skills and compare it with those that you will need to complete the project. Discuss ways to overcome the shortfalls (learn on your own, hire expertise, use school or company facilities, etc.).

5. Refer back to three user groups you identified in b. above. What are their needs, desires, and mental maps? What mix of effect, affect and navigational efficiency will be most effective in appealing to each user group?

F u r t h e r   R e a d i n g

● Berger, Dale E., Kathy Pezdek, and William P. Banks, eds., *Applications of Cognitive Psychology: Problem Solving, Education, and Computing.* Hillsdale, N.J.: Erlbaum Publishing, 1987.

● Chase, W. J., and Herbert A. Siman. "Perception in Chess." *Cognitive Psychology* 4 (January 1972): 55-81.

● March, James G. "Bounded Rationality, Ambiguity, and the Engineering of Choice." *Rand Journal of Economics* 9, no. 2 (Autumn 1978): 587-608. Abstract located at http://www.rand.org/misc/rje/abstracts/abstracts/./1978/Autumn_1978_pp._587_60 8.html

● Mason, Richard O., and Conger, Sue A., "Systems Analysis" in the *Encyclopedia of Operations Research and Management Science*, edited by Saul Gass and Carl Harris, Newell, Mass.: Kohler Academic Publishers, 1996.

PREPARATION

Part 2

PREPARATION

Web presentation design is conducted in several basic phases: preparation, design, implementation, and maintenance/continuous improvement. These phases represent the natural sequence and major shifts in thinking that occur during Web presentation development. Keep in mind that although the methods presented are discussed sequentially as they apply to each phase, in practice the phases overlap and are repeated several times before the project is completed.

Part II of this book discusses the processes of **preparation**, the first phase of Web site development. During preparation, the designer establishes the presenter and user purposes, collects materials, generates ideas, identifies the information to be presented, the users, and the users' needs. Preparation includes two closely related processes. First, the research and idea generation process, covered in Chapter 3, describes the period during which the **information domain** is defined, that is, the range of information that will be included in the Web site.

The second process is information analysis and structuring, which is the subject of Chapter 4. During information analysis, the information domain is broken down into individual pieces of information called chunks. During information structuring, the information chunks are reassembled to reflect their interrelationships in an information structure diagram.

3

Research and Idea Generation

In This Chapter You Will Learn To:

- Use two approaches to information domain definition—user centered and information centered
- Move back and forth between user- and information-centered analysis to better define the information domain
- Apply several methods of data collection: brainstorming, interviewing, virtual value chain analysis, and Web researching

W e b   D e s i g n   i n   t h e   R e a l   W o r l d

Best Personalized Books

At their last meeting, Jack, Wendy, Sue, and Dick had agreed on two user groups the Best Web site would serve: individuals already licensed by Best, and individuals who in viewing the site might be interested in getting licensed. The task now was to decide what information these user groups would want. As they worked on this during the course of several meetings, however, they kept coming back to one group of potential users they thought they had decided to eliminate: individual book buyers. Was there a way to work them into the Web site without infringing on the business of their licensed customers? Meanwhile, Sue remained concerned that putting too many restrictions on the information available to potential licensees would discourage them.

Overview: Research and Idea Generation

The main goal during research and idea generation is to define the users and the information they are likely to need or want. In addition, the presenter's objectives and all of the potential information to be used—ideas, facts, images, prices, and so on—are identified and collected. The products of idea generation are:

- the definition of expected information content for each group of users
- a statement of what the Web presentation will do (that is, its functionality)
- a list of information sources

The totality of information collected forms the Web presentation content, or, as it is more formally called, its information domain. The domain may be rough and loosely specified at the beginning, but it grows, becomes clearer, and takes shape as the project progresses. Several different techniques can be used to define the information domain:

- brainstorming
- interviewing
- virtual value chain analysis
- Web research

Brainstorming is the informal, nonjudgmental development of as many ideas as can be generated. **Interviewing** is the questioning of experts to obtain the needed information. **Virtual value chain analysis** is the analysis of the process a company uses to provide a service or create and sell a product. Its goal is to determine which aspects of the process can be transported to the Web, thereby providing the customer with added value. **Web research** is purposeful surfing to evaluate other sites for desirable hyperlinks, to locate interesting designs, and/or to get information on competitors' sites. Later in this chapter we discuss each of these techniques in detail.

Key Roles

Information stewards play the key role in idea generation. They know the most about the possible users, the information that those users would most likely want, and the information available to be put on the site.

The designers are usually the interviewers, and the stewards or presenters are the interviewees. Designers are like sponges during this stage of Web development, absorbing information from a variety of sources that they discover themselves or that they are provided with by information stewards. Designers participate in generating ideas, drawing on their information systems backgrounds to guide brainstorming sessions and interviews with stewards. They can help stewards clarify their ideas by asking probing questions and make sure the information elicited is complete in terms of its content and functionality.

Defining the Information Domain

At the beginning of a project, the boundaries of the information domain are usually quite general and vague. Defining the information domain presents a kind of chicken-and-egg dilemma. To define all relevant information, stewards and designers need to know who all the possible users and surfers are and what their wants and needs might be. But to figure out who the users are, the stewards and designers need to know what kind of information the organization has available to offer. To resolve this problem, designers and stewards begin with rough definitions of all categories of information in the information domain and the using audience, then cycle back and forth, refining the definitions of each until they are specific enough to identify groups of targeted information users and their actions.

One approach to defining the information domain might concentrate on answering the question, "Who are the users?" Another approach might be to focus on the question, "What information should the Web presentation contain?" These two different approaches are known as **user centered** and **information centered**, respectively. It is best to use both methods to develop a complete understanding of all potential Web uses. In both approaches the final result is a definition of groups of users and the information and functions that will be provided for them on the Web. The difference between them is in the order of definition.

In the **user-centered approach**, the first step is to identify each user group. The next is to determine the type of information each group might want and the type of actions they might take. Figure 3-1 lists user groups typical of different types of Web presentations—intranet, Internet, and extranet. Intranet users are within the organization and are likely to take actions around changing jobs, questioning company experts, or accessing company information. Internet user groups, recall from Chapter 2, might be customers, prospects, stockholders, the media, and so on. Their needs differ substantially from those of employees. Finally, extranet users are companies in the presenting organization's value chain: vendors, suppliers, and customers. The needs of these three user groups may overlap, and sorting out which information to present where becomes a topic for consideration.

Potential User Group	Internet/Web	Intranet	Extranet
General public	X		
News media	X		
Board of directors	X	X	X
Customers	X		X
Vendors	X		X
Stockholders	X		
Job applicants	X		
Employees	X	X	X

Figure 3-1   User groups served from different networks

In the **information-centered approach**, specific topics or categories of information are identified. First, each type of information in the organization is defined in general terms (for instance, product descriptions). Usually, each information type relates to an organizational department. Finance has financial information, sales has customer order information, and so on, as shown in Figure 3-2. From the general list in the figure, information that might be desired or useful to potential surfers and users is identified.

Here, then, the process of integrating information from the user-centered and information-centered approaches begins. Designers identify the users to whom the information available would most appeal. They might also ask and answer these general questions:

- What do potential users want to know about our company?
- What do we want users to know about us?
- What might Web users want to ask about our company and its business?
- How might a Web user interact with our company?

Drawing from the potential groups of users identified by means of the user-centered approach, designers then match potential information chunks and functions with groups of users likely to want that information and to use those functions. **Functionality** refers to exactly what the Web pages will *do*. For instance, a Web presentation might allow the user to place an order or request specific information. Once the information is acquired from the user, some issues to be dealt with include: What should be done with the information? Where should it be stored? Does the user require a response?

These are all potential functions to be defined, not necessarily in detail at this point, but enough to determine any related, parallel activities that might need to occur. No matter what the starting point—users or information—the result is the same. *The goal is to define the users, the information they are likely to want, and the functions they are likely to use.*

Information Type	Internet	Intranet	Extranet
Company policies and procedures	Some	X	Some
Inventory		X	X
Job openings	X	X	
Manufacturing plans and status		X	X
New product information	X	X	X
Order processing	X	X	X
Product specifications/descriptions	X	X	X
Purchasing information	X	X	X
Shipping information	X	X	X
Stock value, price, history, and trends	X	X	X

Figure 3-2   Company information availability

When the user and information definitions are complete, there's a need to look more closely at each category of information in the domain. What are the sources of this information (that is, where is it located)? It might be found in different departments in a single division, similar departments in different divisions, and so on. It's also important to know what format the information is in. Information can exist in a variety of forms, or media: electronic text, pamphlets, photographs, reports, drawings, audio, video, or film.

All possible sources of information in all kinds of media should be identified by designers and information stewards, who will then review their findings to determine which will provide the most complete and accurate information about a given topic area. Having this information, the designers also can choose the most convenient and timely means for converting it into a format that is usable on the Web.

Further Defining the Information Domain

Defining the information domain can be a complex and lengthy process. Some techniques that move the process along include helping to generate new ideas (brainstorming), uncovering additional information (interviewing), filtering out inappropriate information (value chain analysis), and providing access to sites already on the Web that are sponsored by comparable organizations (Web research.)

Brainstorming

Brainstorming is an activity that encourages creative thinking as a means of generating as many ideas as possible in a short period of time. It is an effective method for identifying information to be included in Web sites. Brainstorming encourages the sharing of outrageous and wild ideas to develop solutions to problems, identify Web content, identify information sources, or identify issues to be resolved.

It occurs when a meeting or session is arranged to bring all the participants together to discuss a topic. A moderator is assigned to facilitate the discussion. The moderator sets ground rules, introduces the topic for brainstorming, and provides any background information that might be useful to the participants. The general ground rule is that no judgmental comments or criticisms of any type are allowed during the idea generation phase. The first part of a session is when most of the brainstorming occurs. The group is asked to generate ideas on the subject topic. The moderator then lists all ideas the group generates in a place that is clearly visible to the participants. In the second part of the session, each idea is discussed and evaluated in enough detail to determine whether or not it is worth pursuing further. If an idea is kept, it is assigned to one or more of the participants for follow-up work to refine it, locate information sources, define alternatives, define competition, and so on.

Interviewing

Interviewing is the process of asking questions and getting responses. Interviews can have a single interviewer and a single respondent, or they can have many participants with one or a few interviewers. In interviews conducted during the preparation phase of Web presentations, the designers are usually the interviewers, and the stewards and/or presenters are the interviewees. Group interviews can be very productive because many minds focused on a single set of questions can generate more perspectives than one-on-one interviews can. In addition, conflicts, issues needing resolution, and inconsistencies can be identified easily. Group interviews work best with groups of fewer than 15 people. Interviews can be used to elicit all kinds of information, quantitative or qualitative.

The quality of the interview results depends on the skills of the interviewer. Developing the right questions and posing them in an effective manner is an art that is achieved through practice. Interviews can produce biased results if the interviewer asks questions in a prejudicial manner, for example, "You agree with the statement . . . , don't you?" assumes a "yes" answer even though the person may not agree.

Interviews frequently require multiple sessions with several people to verify the accuracy of results and to resolve conflicting information. Also, interviews are always subject to political responses that further the self-interest of a respondent; skepticism is a useful trait in an interviewer, and cross-checking is a necessity.

Interviews can cover a wide variety of topics ranging from the very broad to the very narrow. Broad interviews are usually conducted using open-ended questions, that is, questions for which there are numerous possible answers. Narrow interviews usually focus on a single topic and look for specific responses using closed-ended questions.

Interviews also can vary in the extent to which they are structured. Structured interviews are interviews in which the same set of questions with little variation is asked of all respondents. Structured interviews are useful for obtaining a more objective evaluation of answers to questions,

3

CHAPTER

they require less training on the part of the interviewer, and they are generally shorter in duration than unstructured interviews. They also can cost more to prepare because of the time and effort required to develop effective questions. Moreover, they can sound mechanical and can suppress information if follow-up questions are not allowed.

Unstructured interviews, on the other hand, are interviews in which the same starting questions might be asked, but in which follow-up questions are developed during the interview based on the response obtained, not on a predefined set of questions. Unstructured interviews give the interviewer the greatest flexibility but require great attention to what is said and can be difficult to conduct. When not well run, unstructured interviews can waste time, alienate participants, generate irrelevant information, and produce results that are difficult to analyze.

While there is no one right way to conduct an interview, most interviews proceed from general, open-ended questions to specific, closed-ended questions and are unstructured. Many interviewers like to end with the open-ended questions, "Is there anything else we haven't covered or that you think we should know?" At the beginning of a project, when designers know the least about the information domain, unstructured interviews with open-ended questions obtain the most information in the least amount of time. As designers become better acquainted with the information domain, their questions become more specific and closed, and the interviews tend to be more structured, too.

In conducting any type of interview, planning always results in a more productive session. Successful interviews generally include the steps shown in Figure 3-3.

1. Prepare an agenda and small (under five) set of topics.
2. Set an appointment with the interviewee(s).
3. Provide a list of topics to be covered and give an maximum meeting duration.
4. Prepare at least the initial set of questions to be asked.
5. Arrive at the interview on time, if not a bit early.
6. Introduce yourself (if you have not previously met the interviewee) and define your role on the Web project team.
7. Begin the interview with the initial set of questions, paying close attention to responses, making notes, and creating follow-up questions.
8. Probe for details as required.
9. Use a planned closing statement that summarizes the main points of each topic.
10. Identify any follow-up activities with dates for completion and responsible individuals.
11. Make detailed notes of the results immediately after the interview.
12. Send a copy of the notes to the interviewee(s). Ask that the summary be reviewed for accuracy, and that any comments be returned to you by a set date.

Figure 3-3   Steps to a successful interview show that planning and follow-through are important

Virtual Value Chain Analysis

A Web presentation is intended to provide both the customer and the company with added value, and often this added value is most measurable when some aspect of the company's products or services are obtainable online via the Web presentation. Remember, the information domain is not just limited to chunks of information. The information domain can also contain more tangible items, such as products or services. The technique of virtual value chain analysis is the most effective in identifying such aspects of the information domain. It involves the analysis of the company's current process for providing a service or for creating and selling a product.

The steps to evaluating what parts of a business process can be offered as part of the information domain are:

1. Determine each product or service to be offered via the Web. Qualifying product criteria might include low cost, uniqueness, or ability to fill a market niche. The information stewards or marketing personnel responsible for each product line will be able to help direct the qualifying process.

2. Determine the company's competitive stance with the product or service. A company can establish a leading competitive position by being the first to market with a new product, using radically new technologies, developing a capacity for continual innovation, or wisely investing substantial money in its technology infrastructure.

3. Evaluate the current, real-world value chain for each product or service to determine which activities can be carried out successfully online.

Depending on the information and functionality users need, there are three basic levels at which a company can offer, as part of the information domain, products and services online. At level 1, it can automate the way business information is processed and received; at level 2, it can automate the way the customer receives information or services; and at level 3, it can offer a completely new service to customers, one that can be offered only via the Web.

Federal Express is a company whose Web presentation has evolved to gradually achieve each of these levels. In the 1980s, overnight delivery services such as FedEx knew when they received a package and when it was delivered. Facing stiff competition, FedEx reevaluated its business processes and determined that many customers wanted to know where in the delivery process a package was, especially when it was not delivered as expected. FedEx reached the first level of use by making such information available to its customers.

To do this, the company first sought to automate the extensive information by including truck loading, driver delivery, and customer signature on a hand-held computer. The hand-held computers plugged into a dashboard radio device that transmitted the signature and delivery information within seven seconds to the centralized FedEx database in Memphis, Tennessee. Customers could access this information by calling a toll-free number and speaking to a customer service representative to learn, to the minute, where their packages were in transit.

FedEx moved to the second level when it made its package delivery database available on the Web to its customers. This allowed users to determine the status of any of their packages. The move was taken to reduce demands on the customer service department, but it had the added effect of increasing business by 15% almost immediately, while at the same time reducing the cost of customer service dramatically. This shift had several other subtle effects. FedEx was now viewed as being the innovator in the package delivery industry. Even though its shipment process was unchanged, the Web-based information process enhanced the company's image. A secondary effect was to reduce the threat from all competitors simply because they initially could not offer the same service and, if they did, they would clearly be doing so in response to FedEx's innovation.

FedEx reached the third and highest level of Web service when it began to offer customers VirtualOrder. VirtualOrder is a service through which FedEx develops and maintains a Web site for the customer. The Web site manages its ordering and shipping activities—doing the shipping, of course, via FedEx. Delivering value in new ways by developing new business processes in the virtual world that have no analogue in the real world is the key characteristic of the third level of Web service. The customer must supply its company and product information and give FedEx access to its inventory.

Web Research

Frequently, you will be stuck for ideas or unsure about how to use some piece of information. Doing research on information and sites already on the Web can help. Web research can be done using books, magazines, and other print materials found in the library or, more commonly, on the Web itself.

A **search engine** is a software program that allows a user to submit criteria that will help to locate a specific set of information on the Web. The search engine uses these criteria to compile something called an **information query**, which is a question that asks for the URLs of all sites that contain the desired information. The engine then retrieves from its entire index of sites a listing of those sites that appear to meet the particular search criteria. Each site in that list is called a **hit**. There are more than 30 search engines now on the Web, and more appear online regularly. Figure 3-4 lists the addresses for a number of popular search engines, all of which have similar information query capabilities. You might ask if we need all of these engines; the answer is that, right now, it doesn't hurt to have them. Different engines provide indexes with different sorts of information, so no one engine is good for all inquiries.

Search Engine URL	Type of Search
http://www.100hot.com	100 Hot Sites
http://www.altavista.digital.com	General
http://www.bigbook.com	Business Names, Addresses
http://www.bigfoot.com	Individual Names, Addresses, Email
http://www.dogpile.com	Multiple search engine results at once
http://www.dreamscape.com/frankvad	Free software, etc.
http://www.excite.com	General
http://www.hotbot.com	Names, Addresses
http://www.infoseek.com	General
http://www.lycos.com	General
http://www.nln.com	Multiple general search engines
http://www.opentext.net	General based on document contents
http://www.search.com	General
http://www.shareware.com	Free software
http://www.whowhere.com	Individual, Government Names, Addresses
http://www.worldpages.com	Global Names, Addresses, Email
http://www.yahoo.com	General

Figure 3-4   Popular search engines

Three strategies for searching are by keyword (for instance, secondary school), by subject (education), and by URL (www. hwssb.edu.on.ca/stjoachi/). Another technique is to use intelligent agent software. You supply the agent program with topics that interest you, and it searches the Web for these topics regularly and sends them to your terminal automatically. Another name for this software, because of its automatic delivery of information, is **push technology**. One such program is Pointcast, which is similar to a newspaper-clipping service. These agents will become more popular and sophisticated in the years to come.

To use a search engine, perform the following general steps:

1.   Log onto the Web.

2.   Enter a URL to access one of the engine addresses.

3.   Enter the criteria for your search.

4.   Notice the total number of hits that are listed (most search engines will give you a total for the number of sites retrieved for a particular search; this number can range from one or two to several million).

5.   Narrow and *re*-search as needed by adding criteria and resubmitting the request (explained below).

6.   Review and go to one or more of the sites returned to determine which ones meet your needs.

7.   Use the information and sites or reformulate the search as needed.

In doing research relating to Best Personalized Books, the Web site development team searched for the term "personalized books." The search engines Lycos, AltaVista, and Open Text each responded differently, as shown in Figure 3-5, with some intersecting pages retrieved. Notice that the number of hits (responses) is completely different with each search engine. These differences are due partially to the method used to create index entries. When the index is **active**, the organization employs software programs called **spiders,** which actively search for new sites to add to the index. When the index is **passive**, the organization simply accepts information submitted by managers of other Web sites.

If you get a few thousand hits, you need to narrow your search. If you are new to using search engines, you will probably need to do some practice searches until you have a feel for the one or two search engines that give you the best results. In the case of the Best Web team's searches, AltaVista came up with about 200,000 hits—clearly an unmanageable number. Lycos came up with thousands of hits at close to 5,000—still a lot. Open Text, on the other hand, listed 136 hits, a number that the team could take the time to explore. (*Remember that the smallest number of hits is no guarantee that they're the best or most appropriate.*)

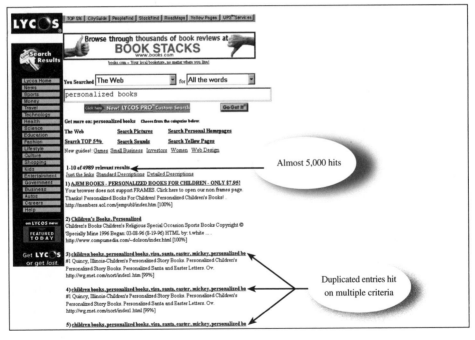

Figure 3-5   Differing search engine results

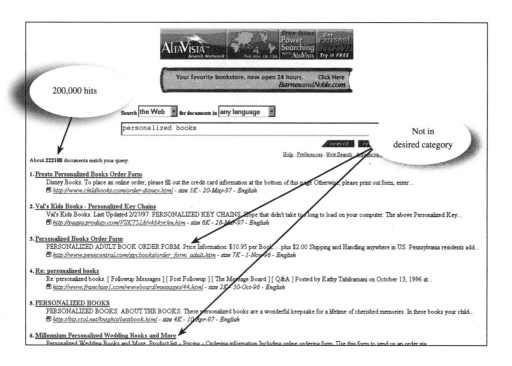

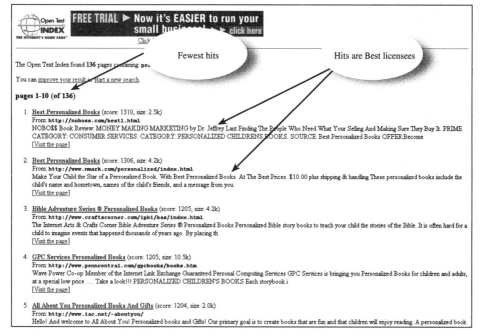

Figure 3-5 (continued)

Each search engine allows custom narrowing of criteria to reduce the number of hits. Each responds to searches that use **Boolean logic**, that is, searches that combine the words searched for with the terms AND, OR, or NOT. These terms, called **Boolean operators**, together with strategic use of parentheses, can be used to connect different search criteria. For instance, to narrow the search for Best competitors, we might enter the following:

```
((personalized AND books) OR (business AND opportunity)) AND children
```

This query asks the search engine to list sites in which it can find the entries "personalized books" OR "business opportunities" that also contain the word "children." Initially, three sets of responses will be developed—one set for "personalized" and "books" together, one set for "business" and "opportunity" together, and one set with the word "children". Then, the final criterion is applied to identify those URLs from the first two sets that are also in the third set. The same three search engines were asked this query. The results, in Figure 3-6, show that Open Text conducted the most precise search and came up with a small number of hits that came the closest to the information wanted. The AltaVista search increased to more than 1.5 million hits as a result of adding the "business opportunities" choice and because it returns entries that match any single word. It would need major retooling to obtain good results. Lycos dropped the number of hits pretty sharply, but Open Text still came up with the closest matches.

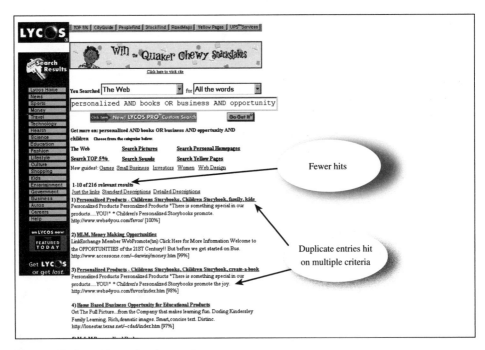

Figure 3-6   Narrowing the search

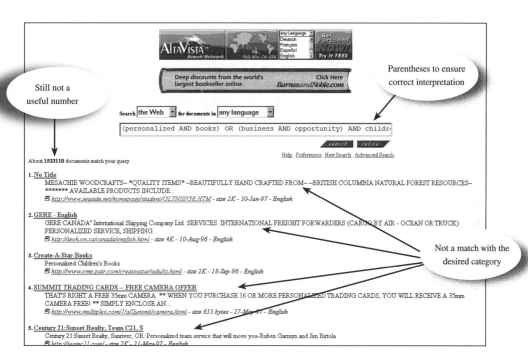

Figure 3-6 (continued)

W e b   D e s i g n   i n   t h e   R e a l   W o r l d

Best Personalized Books

To determine the information domain for Best's Web site, Sue and Dick needed to learn more detailed information about the personalized book business and the way Best dealt with its customers. They spent several meetings interviewing Jack and Wendy. During these sessions, Sue asked very broad, open-ended questions, such as, "Tell me about your business" and "What are all of the ways you deal with your licensees?" and "How does someone become a licensee?"

As the meetings proceeded, the questions became more specific: "How many licensees use the Internet?" "How many toll-free calls do you get a day?" "What proportion of information phone calls result in a license sale?" "What is the growth rate in toll-free calls?" While the specific answers to these questions are proprietary to Best, Sue and Dick used the answers to guide the Web site design, keeping in mind that the goal was to reduce the number of toll-free phone calls to Best and to automate as many activities as possible on the Web.

Two specific issues that the team still had to resolve were whether to give individual book buyers access to the site and how much access to give potential licensees. Several rounds of user-centered and information-centered discussions helped them arrive at a solution. Ultimately, the team decided to give individuals the opportunity to buy books

through the Web site. Brainstorming was used to find acceptable solutions after the issues were identified. Jack's main concern was avoiding competition with the licensees. Sue's concern was to provide book buyers with purchase capabilities. Finally, both Wendy and Jack wanted to make sure their business as licensors was clearly presented; any confusion could have legal or tax consequences.

To begin generating some ideas, Sue asked the following: Assume that book buying by single individuals is allowed. How can we do this without causing other problems?

The first suggestion by Jack, who was still not convinced on the idea, was to take the potential book buyer's name, address, and phone information, then give it to a licensee. Sue asked why automated sending of information couldn't be done. Then Jack realized both how many individual buyers were out there and how information on their geographic locations would provide valuable marketing information. He also thought that having a letter accompany the request would be nice. Sue observed that the requests could be forwarded with a letter to a licensee and copied to the main office, automated by a Web site application program. In addition, statistics could be compiled on individual purchase requests and their dispositions to appease any legal or tax audits.

Individuals would be able to order books by completing an interactive form available on the Web site. But rather than having Best fill the orders, it would review and then forward them to licensed sellers. Orders from countries outside the U.S. would be referred to licensees based in the particular country, and orders from within the U.S. would be distributed randomly. This solution made for a win-win-win strategy for Best, for licensees, and for the buyer. Best would demonstrate its largesse, not only in not competing with licensees but in giving them business; the licensee got a "free" sale; and the buyer could do one-stop shopping—completing an order after browsing the site.

It also took a lot of brainstorming and discussion to settle the question of how much information to make available to potential licensees. Jack and Wendy needed more convincing that the potential licensees were an important user group. Sue was concerned that potential licensees would be put off by the requirement to phone Best's 800 number if they wanted more information than was available at the Web site. It seemed too bureaucratic for a Web-site literate surfer. Wendy argued that the phone call was a good way to determine the motivation level of the person. Both positions seemed reasonable and defensible. The stalemate on the decision was revisited several times before it was resolved.

Finally, the team decided on an interactive query form for potential licensees. The query form would provide a form of closure to a thread regarding license inquiries. (*Closure*, a term that will be introduced more

formally in Chapter 4, refers to the completion of an activity—in this case, the pursuit of an interest in becoming a licensee.) Automating the query was important to appeal to the targeted surfers interested in becoming licensees, by allowing them to use the Web (or phone, as preferred) as a means of contacting Best. The various contracts and forms needed to set up shop would not be presented on the Web, but users would be able to order them electronically. At first the Kalishers were reluctant to go along with this option. After asking a number of questions to uncover the reason for this reluctance, Sue and Dick realized that Jack and Wendy didn't have a clear understanding about how interactive forms worked.

A walk-through of the process, using a paper model of a possible query screen design, gave Jack and Wendy the information they needed to make their decision. As shown in Figure 3-7, the query form would identify the name and address of the requester, the kind of information the requester desired, and the form of mailing desired. The form also provides a free-form space where users can type in comments and/or make nonstandard requests.

The plan was to have an application program developed to read the file once a day and process requests. Processing for a standard request included creation of a mailing label and bill of lading for the materials requested. These items would be delivered to the shipping area for assembly and shipping. A listing of all standard requests plus any free-form comments would be printed for follow-up by the marketing staff.

This, too, was an innovative, win-win solution. Best restricted the amount of information it would give out over the Web, while users would be able to get the information they wanted without taking the extra step of making a phone call. Of course, there was still the question of making contracts, forms, and certain company information directly available to licensees at the Web site. This problem was eventually solved by creating a two-screen design, one for nonlicensees (the general public) and one for licensees, which they could access with a password.

Another part of the learning process for Sue and Dick was to look through every piece of printed marketing and advertising material Best had available. They discovered that the promotional materials reflected the rich graphic content of the books themselves. This meant they would be able to use many of the materials "as is," which would simplify the design job. A number of the brochures were also a good source of descriptive copy.

Samples from a Best brochure are pictured in Figure 3-8. They show the basic steps involved in creating a book. The layout is interesting, the wording is clear and concise, and the pictures complete the user's understanding of what needs to be done to create a book.

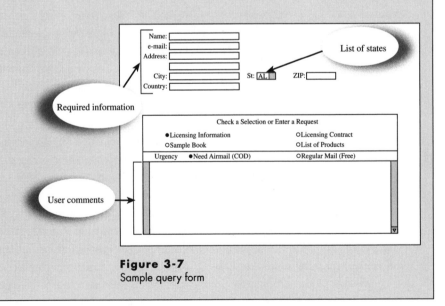

Figure 3-7
Sample query form

The information domain that resulted from the research and idea generation process for Best also included the following:

- List of books—including cover graphics and plot lines
- Explanation of why Best is best
- List of frequently asked questions
- Company listing addresses, locations, and Best contact information

- Company newsletters
- Letter of recognition from President Clinton
- Testimonials from licensees
- *Inc.* article placing Best as 167th on the magazine's list of fastest growing small companies in the United States

Step 1:
Type the child's name and other pertinent information into the computer. Place the illustrated pages in the laser printer and print.

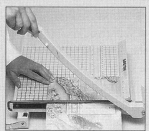

Step 2:
Cut or fold the pages in half.

Step 3:
Staple the pages together with the adhesive sheets on top and bottom.

Step 4:
Attach the stapled pages to the hard cover and you're finished in less than 3 minutes!

Figure 3-8
Samples from Best brochure

S u m m a r y

Information-centered and user-centered approaches to idea generation can both be used to define the information domain of the Web presentation. Both methods lead to the same result. The information domain is the totality of information collected during the research and idea generation process that is to be used to develop the Web presentation.

Four commonly used techniques of information domain definition are brainstorming, interviewing, virtual value chain analysis, and Web research. In brainstorming, participants first identify as many alternative ideas on the subject as possible. During the idea generation phase of the brainstorming session, no judgments or opinions on the ideas are allowed. When the list of ideas appears sufficient, each is discussed and either elaborated for follow-up or discarded as not useful.

Interviewing is a method of obtaining information by asking questions of participants. Questions range from completely open-ended, having no single answer, to completely closed-ended, having either a yes or no answer. Interviews also can range from structured, with the same questions asked of all interviewees, to unstructured, with most question development taking place at each interview and customized to the answers given. At the end of a good interview, the participants should have a review of information exchanged, and all should know if they have any follow-up work to perform.

Virtual value chain analysis analyzes the real world business processes and information used in support of these processes to determine which can be mirrored in the virtual world. Not all real world work has a virtual alternative. That which does requires careful design to enhance real world activities.

Web research is purposeful surfing that uses search engines to find relevant materials from sites already on the World Wide Web. Boolean logic that connects a keyword with "AND" and "OR" alternatives is used to develop queries. The search engine returns results in order either by most applicable hits or by most frequent access.

The outcome of the idea generation process is a detailed definition of the following:

- the goal of the Web presentation
- user groups
- actions to be taken on information or by users
- information domain
- information sources

R e v i e w   Q u e s t i o n s

1. Compare and contrast user-centered and information-centered approaches to defining Web site content.

2. Describe the differences between brainstorming and interviewing as methods of defining Web site content.

3. What are the strengths and weaknesses of brainstorming?

4. What are the strengths and weaknesses of structured interviews?

5. When are structured interviews a better technique than unstructured interviews for obtaining desired information?

6. What are three uses for Web research?

7. What approach (user-centered or information-centered) to Web site development would be more appropriate for the Library of Congress and why? What about PepsiCo? What about a small entrepreneurial company selling golf balls? If you don't know enough about the Library of Congress or PepsiCo to answer these questions, visit their Web sites and take a look.

8. Create and execute a query to find information on a Fortune 500 company's most recent annual report.

9. Using the steps to virtual value chain analysis, define what type of information your school or organization might put on the Web for one functional area.

P r o j e c t s

1. Surf the Web for three of the search engines in Figure 3-4 (for instance, http://www.lycos.com). Determine the extent of the larger body of knowledge, facts, data, on one line and information from which each page was abstracted. To what extent were the pages a rehash of facts or a creative development of new ideas? Create a report on your findings.

2. Repeat project 1 on a university site you choose from http://www.edunet.com and compare it with the Web site sponsored by your school or organization. If your organization doesn't have a Web site, select two schools on Edunet.

3. Use http://www.dogpile.com to look up information about your family. Which site provides the best map to your parents' or your house? How do you feel about the use of your personal information without your permission?

C a s e   P r o j e c t

 1. List all information sources you expect to draw on to complete your project. Organize them by type of source—interview, published reports, unpublished memos or other written materials, public sources (e.g., *Business Week* articles), corporate sources (e.g., product specification brochures), automated databases, etc. This is your preliminary information domain. Review your project work assignments for the previous chapters and revise them based on what you now know. For example, do you have all the information needed from the involved information stewards? Update the definition of the project's goals and the nature of the Web presentation.

 2. Perform a Web search using http://www.dogpile.com to locate information already on the Web that relates to your Web site development in question 1 above. Compare the results from each search engine. Narrow the search as needed to get to a useful number of sites. Go to those sites and assess their definitions of "users" and information contents. Which search engine provided the best results? Which provided a usable number of sites the fastest? Print the screens of your searches to document the results of this activity.

F u r t h e r   R e a d i n g

- McKibbon, William. *The Age of Missing Information*. New York: Penguin Books, 1992.
- Senechal, Anne. "It's All in the Process." *Adobe Magazine* 8, no. 4 (Spring 1997): 34–40.
- Raport, Jeffrey, and John Sviokla. "Managing the Virtual Value Chain." *Harvard Business Review*, December 1995, 1–12.
- Sullivan, Danny, and Richard Karpinski. "Supercharge Your Web Searches," *Netguide*, May 1997, 63–74. Visit the *Netguide* Web site at http://www.netguidemag.com

4

Information Decomposition and Information Structuring

In This Chapter You Will Learn To:

- Decompose information into its component information objects, or chunks
- Reduce information to its simplest form
- Structure information objects based on the presenter's business needs and users' information needs
- Depict information objects in an information structure diagram
- Describe cardinality and volatility, two attributes of information objects
- Describe three types of relationships shared by information objects
- Test the information structure for its logic and ease of use

W e b   D e s i g n   i n   t h e   R e a l   W o r l d

Best Personalized Books

Once the information domain for Best's Web presentation had been established, Sue and Dick needed to break it down into individual pieces of information. These pieces of information could be reorganized to reflect both their relationship to one another and the way a user might logically access and move through the information.

After carefully reviewing all the information sources they had collected (brochures, sample books, etc.), they broke the information down into the outline shown in Figure 4-1. Sue and Dick's first goal was

Company information
      Introductory information
      Background & history (includes growth statistics)
      Awards
      Distinctive competency — unique patented technology, growing product lines
         with licensing arrangements with Disney, etc.
      Emphasis on quality
      Multilingual products
      4 reasons why Best is best
Testimonials of successful licensees
The process of creating a book (what a licensee does)
Languages of books
Product samples
Buy a book — form
      Customer identifying information
      Item type
      Custom personalization information form
Become a licensee
      Computer requirements
      Licensing procedure
      The process of creating a book (what a licensee does)
      Best company support
Marketing support
      Marketing support products
      Selling techniques
Existing licensee support
      Marketing support
         Marketing support products
         Selling techniques
      Product samples
      Purchasing — form for product purchase
         Security information
         Purchase form (automatically displays licensee
            name/address information and any pre-arranged
            financing information)

Figure 4-1
Best information outline

to make sure that they had included all relevant information. This information would be
the lifeblood of Best's Web site, and they
wanted to make sure it was complete. Their
next goal was to organize the information
into main topics and subtopics, thereby introducing the different levels of detail that
would be worked into the Web site. While
the outline technique is not a requirement at
this stage of Web site development, it is a
helpful organizing tool when the designers
are new to the information domain—as were
Sue and Dick.

Overview: Information Decomposition and Structuring

Some Web presentations are pleasing to view, but their presentation of information is confusing.
They look nice, but you can't find the information you think is there. When you look for a piece of
information, it is buried in an obscure place in the presentation and is often incomplete. At other
sites, you may find it easy to find the information you want. What constitutes a well-organized site?
How is it achieved? The answers lie in how well the designer performed the activities of information decomposition and structuring. These activities provide the foundation for the organization of
information in a Web site.

Decomposition is the separation of something into its parts. In developing Web presentations,
decomposition is the process of separating the information identified in the research and idea generation phase into its component parts, thereby creating a set of information objects. As mentioned
previously, an **information object** is any fully defined unit of information that expresses a single,
complete thought as perceived by the viewer. Each information object (also called a **chunk**) eventually
results in a Web page element. Ideally, object definition results in a set of objects with two characteristics: the objects are **mutually exclusive**—that is, the content of any one object does not overlap with
the content of any other object—and they are **collectively exhaustive** of the full body of ideas developed—that is, the objects represent all the information contained in the information domain—nothing
has been overlooked.

Once the decomposition of the information domain is complete, information structuring can begin.
The overall intent of information structuring is to create a map of the information objects that serves
two basic needs: that of the presenter and that of the user. Recall from Chapter 1 that it is not only different types of users who will have different expectations of a Web site; *presenters* also have their
distinct ideas of what the site should accomplish. The organization of information objects presented in
Figure 4-1 reflects Jack and Wendy's vision of the site. Various groups of users—such as potential
book buyers and current licensees—will be looking for something else, as shown in the outlines in
Figure 4-2. These two outlines present information in ways that are likely to satisfy these two user
groups. Outlines are a convenient way to get a handle on the expectations of different user groups.

GO to... the sites for Fairfax County, VA, and Summit County, OH, **http://www.co.fairfax.va.us** and **http://www.neo.lrun.com/ City_of_Akron/**, and compare them. Which site is more useful? Which is better organized and why? Note your criticisms of each site for comparison with your own presentation.

Information decomposition and structuring helps designers manage complex and voluminous information efficiently. The goal of these activities is documentation of an information structure that is used first as the basis for Web design, and second as the basis for the maintenance, redesign, and updating of the Web presentation.

Key Roles

Information stewards and designers are partners in information decomposition. Designers know more about the process of decomposition simply because their job as designer requires that they do it all the time. Information stewards know more about their information domain and therefore know when a decomposition of their information domain is accurate and complete. Stewards and designers work together, with equal responsibility, to decompose information into its objects and to figure out which user groups will be interested in which objects. The process of structuring the information for the Web site and then documenting this structure is carried out by the designer, although information stewards offer guidance along the way and must approve the final information structure.

Potential Book Buyers' View
Languages of books
Product samples
Buy a book — form
    Customer identifying information
    Item type
    Customizing information (child, pet, friend, and relative names)

Current Licensee View
Purchasing — form for product purchase
    Purchase form (automatically displays licensee
        name/address information and any pre-arranged
        financing information)
Newsletters — current & future plans, notices, etc.
Marketing support
    Marketing support products
    Selling techniques
Product samples
Languages of books
Company information
    Growth statistics
    Awards
    Distinctive competency — unique patented technology, growing product lines,
        licensing arrangements with various organizations, etc.
    Quality statistics

Figure 4-2   Differing expectations of users

Information Decomposition Guidelines

Decomposition breaks down general information from the information domain into information objects. The result is a list or outline of a set of fully decomposed objects. Full decomposition results in **atomic information objects** (information in its simplest form); each object has a distinct identity and cannot be further divided without changing or losing its identity. Marketing information, for example, might be an original information object that in later analyses is decomposed into sales support and product support information. Product support information might then be decomposed, for Best products, for instance, into support for books, clocks, and letters, all of which are atomic information objects. All of these objects—from the highest level to the atomic level—are then outlined once to the advantage of the presenter and once to the advantage of *each group* of users, the goal being to meet the expected wants and needs of the presenter and of each and every user group.

An information object may have more than one source. Two sources for the same information object, product advertising, might be the public relations department and the product marketing department. While the PR department advertising focus might be less specific and apply to several products, and the marketing ads might be very specific, both may be sources of publicly available information about a given product. Likewise, each source may be composed of one or more media— text, graphics, video, audio, etc. For instance, advertising might use audio, video, or print media, and the same product (for example, a car) might be presented in each medium. So, in the decomposition process, the ultimate product is a collection of information objects and their sources as captured in a variety of media.

Most text tends to decompose from general to specific information with several layers of intermediate groupings. Figure 4-3 shows the text version of a university (SMU) catalog's description of its international programs.[1] The most general level of information given is the titles of the programs themselves as Semester Programs or Summer Programs. Each program is then broken down by location (SMU-in-Paris and SMU-in-Spain, SMU-in-Japan) and by course (under International Programs Course List). Location is then broken down further to give details on basic requirements and offerings, and the course list is broken down to provide specific course information, including the department offering the course, the course title and ID number, and the time of year. The reader of the catalog progresses from general to more specific information.

1. From the *Southern Methodist University Undergraduate Catalogue*, 1996–1997.

INTERNATIONAL OFFICE

The University offers students an opportunity to live, study, and travel abroad in semester or year-long programs, as well as summer programs. Semester or year-long programs are maintained in Paris, Madrid, Copenhagen, Japan, Britain, Russia, and Australia. The University also offers five-week summer terms in Salzburg, Austria; Oxford and London, England; Rome and Tuscany, Italy; the South of France; Xalapa, Mexico; and Moscow. Programs in other countries may be added from time to time. Instruction in all programs is offered in English, except for courses in foreign languages and literature. Students in good standing at SMU and other universities may participate in SMU's International Programs.

SEMESTER PROGRAMS

SMU-IN-PARIS and SMU-IN-SPAIN. The University has well-established programs in both Paris and Madrid. Participants in SMU-in-Spain should have completed their first year of college-level Spanish. A minimum G.P.A. of 2.70 normally is required. A variety of courses are offered in the following fields: art history, business communications, history, language and literature, political science, and studio art. Students are housed with families. Orientation trips and cultural events are an integral part of both programs. Participation in either program for a full academic year is recommended, but students may attend either the fall or spring semester.

SMU-IN-JAPAN. SMU students have an unusual and challenging opportunity to live and study for the fall or the full academic year through a well-established exchange program with Kwansei Gakuin University, which is located near Osaka, Japan. Students enroll for specially designed courses taught in English. Field trips and cultural events are an integral part of the Japan experience. Students should have completed one year of college Japanese.

SMU-IN-BRITAIN. For students desiring a year of study in England, the University offers counseling and assistance in gaining admission to a British university. For all work successfully completed under this arrangement, appropriate academic credit will be recorded at SMU. In the past, students have studied arts, sciences, engineering, economics, history, and English at various British institutions.

SMU-IN-COPENHAGEN. Through a cooperative agreement with the University of Copenhagen...

SUMMER PROGRAMS

SMU-IN-AUSTRIA. This six-week program allows students to immerse themselves in the Austrian way of life. Students live with Austrian families in Salzburg and study on the grounds of the Leopoldskron Castle, earning six hours of credit. Trips to surrounding areas, including Vienna, are planned.

SMU-IN-LONDON. COMMUNICATIONS. Taking advantage of London as an international center...

INTERNATIONAL PROGRAMS COURSE LIST
F=Fall Semester, S=Spring Semester

SMU-IN-PARIS

Art History
ARHS 3337 Paris Art and Architecture: from 1715
    Through the Present Day (S)
ARHS 3355 Introduction to Impressionism (F)
ARHS 3357 Impressionism in Context (S)

Communications
CCCN 4305 Motion Picture of Paris (F and S)

English
ENGL 3360 Women Writers in Paris (F and S) Or WS 3360

Foreign Literature in Translation
FL 3308 The French Mentality (F and S)
or HIST 3365 Problems in European History or CAPS 3308

French
FREN 1401 (F), 1402 (S) Beginning French (First-year)
FREN 2401 Intermediate French (Second-year) (F and S)
FREN 3355 French Conversation (F)
FREN 3356 Written French (S) . . .

SMU-IN-SPAIN

Art History
ARHS 3345 Great Masters of the Prado Museum (F and S)

Foreign Literature in Translation
FL 3301-02 Spanish Culture and Thought (F and S)
Or SPAN 3373

History
HIST 3365 The Making of Modern Europe: From the
    First World War to the European Community (F)
HIST 3380 Latin American History (S)

Political Science
PLSC 4340 Political History of Contemporary Spain
    (F and S) . . .

Figure 4-3   A college catalogue

Figure 4-4 pulls the information objects out of the catalogue and shows them in outline form, still organized from general to specific. General objects can be said to **own** the specific objects, while specific objects **define** and **give details** relating to general objects.

Some media can capture several information objects in one rendering—a single clip of audio or video can contain many information objects. A spreadsheet, like the one showing the balance sheet for the Conco company in Figure 4-5, can also contain several information objects: one identifying rows

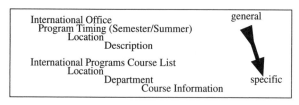

International Office
  Program Timing (Semester/Summer)
    Location
      Description

International Programs Course List
  Location
    Department
      Course Information

general

specific

Figure 4-4   Catalogue information decomposition

(accounts), one identifying columns (years), and one identifying composite information (total assets or growth rate). The more complex the spreadsheet, the more information objects it will contain.

Each information object is often composed of several information objects that represent different topics. In the school catalogue, the information objects are semester/summer, locations, and classes. In the spreadsheet, the assets information object identifies all of the row accounts shown. The steps of decomposition are performed repeatedly to identify each information object and name it. Each source is analyzed to determine the type (or types) of information it contains. The information objects that result from this analysis are then further analyzed and broken down into still more specific information objects. Alternatively, some may be recombined as a single object.

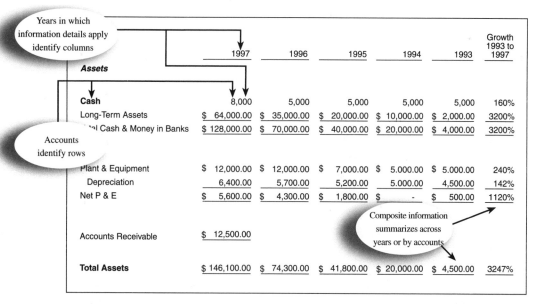

	1997	1996	1995	1994	1993	Growth 1993 to 1997
Assets						
Cash	8,000	5,000	5,000	5,000	5,000	160%
Long-Term Assets	$ 64,000.00	$ 35,000.00	$ 20,000.00	$ 10,000.00	$ 2,000.00	3200%
...al Cash & Money in Banks	$ 128,000.00	$ 70,000.00	$ 40,000.00	$ 20,000.00	$ 4,000.00	3200%
Plant & Equipment	$ 12,000.00	$ 12,000.00	$ 7,000.00	$ 5.000.00	$ 5.000.00	240%
Depreciation	6,400.00	5,700.00	5,200.00	5.000.00	4,500.00	142%
Net P & E	$ 5,600.00	$ 4,300.00	$ 1,800.00	$ -	$ 500.00	1120%
Accounts Receivable	$ 12,500.00					
Total Assets	$ 146,100.00	$ 74,300.00	$ 41,800.00	$ 20,000.00	$ 4,500.00	3247%

Years in which information details apply identify columns

Accounts identify rows

Composite information summarizes across years or by accounts

Figure 4-5   Conco balance sheet

The information objects described in Figure 4-4 begin with the general "International Office" and decompose into "Program Timing," "Location," and "Description." The atomic information object, "Description," contains general information, student requirements, and so on. Similarly, the information objects for the "International Courses" information object decomposes into "Location," "Department," and "Course Information." The atomic-level information object, "Course Information," contains course number, name, and semester offered for every course. In analyzing the outline, location is in both object lists, so the information can be consolidated as shown in Figure 4-6. This type of consolidation is used to minimize duplicated information and to make sure that users, in this case students, can access all information on a subject easily.

```
International Programs
        Timing (Semester/Summer)
                Location
                        Description
                        Department
                                Course Information
```

Figure 4-6   Consolidated catalogue information

This activity of individual information object analysis is repeated until no further divisions of information are possible. As each information object is identified it is also **tracked**, or recorded. The purpose of tracking is to record the "name" or identity of each information object along with an abbreviated description of its basic content. It is also useful to track the object's source. (An object's source may also be referred to as its "origin" or "parentage.") Tracking can be done by means of:

● a list or outline

● a group of 3x5 index cards (with one card for each object)

● a database

The more objects in a Web site, the more elaborate the tracking mechanism becomes. For a small site, such as an individual's set of resume pages, a simple list is sufficient. For the Best Personalized Books site, which resulted in about 100 information objects, the 3x5 cards were used. One of the cards, shown in Figure 4-7, identifies the information object (products, or a list of books), the object contents (a book cover and a plot for each book), some disclaimers, and a code (15, M) to indicate the number of titles listed (15) and the frequency with which they should be reviewed (M, for monthly). For a site with thousands of information objects, a database would be the most effective tracking method. Keeping track of the object's source as well as its contents makes it easier to spot similar information objects (those with the same contents) with different information origins (different sources).

Figure 4-8 shows the decomposition of a resume. On top is the original resume, which is translated into a basic outline, which is in turn broken down into a summary outline. Notice that the summary labels only the higher-level information objects. The atomic information objects contained within them are noted only by their total number. Cheryl Hardesty has had two jobs, so next to the information object labeled "job history" the number 2 appears in parentheses.

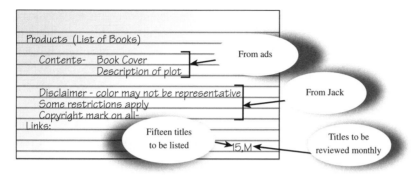

Figure 4-7   Sample tracking method

The summary outline can be created directly from the original document if the information relationships are obvious. In the case of Figure 4-8, both the text from the resume and an interview with its owner were used to complete the information. Depending on the sources of information, other documents and media, as well as other people—that is, stewards—might be involved.

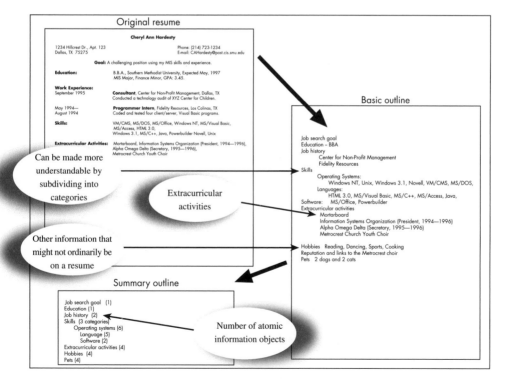

Figure 4-8   Decomposition of a resume

When complete, the outline is reanalyzed to determine if any information objects define the same information. If some information objects *do* define the same information, the sources can be examined to determine which information to use from each. If the information objects *do not* define the same information, then make sure they are identified (named) in such a way that demonstrates their difference.

Compare the summary outline in Figure 4-8 with Figure 4-9. Figure 4-9, which is more lengthy and detailed, is the result of analyzing the resumes of many people in several computer-related industries. The summary outline in Figure 4-8 is the outcome of analysis of the resume of a single person. This comparison shows that both the information objects resulting from an analysis and their structure may differ depending on the number of examples of the information in use, and the number of sources in which the information is found.

```
Identifying information
   Work history
   might be organized by
                  Full- and part-time — or academic and business
                  Duration, company/organization, title, duties
   Skills (for each level of skills in order strongest to weakest)
               Automotive
               Computer
                  Hardware
                           Mainframe
                           Client-server
                           Workstation
                           Other
                  Software
                           Database
                           Telecommunications
                  Languages
               Engineering
                        Mechanical
                        Electrical
                        Other
            Handicraft
            Language
            Machine
   Education
   Honors
               Monetary rewards
   Professional affiliations
               Offices
               Other service
   Veteran status
   Publications
               Refereed
               Nonrefereed
               Invited
               Books
               Other
   Presentations
   Courses taught
   Reviews done for
            Journal list
                     Editorial appointments
            Periodical list
                     Editorial appointments
            Book publisher list
                     Editorial appointments
            Conference list
                     Committee assignments
```

Figure 4-9   Outline based on many resumes

The process of identifying information objects is more an art than a science. One general guideline to remember is that whenever an information object can be broken down into seven or more component objects, a more detailed grouping, possibly with more detailed information objects, should be considered. (Recall the 7 ± 2 rule introduced in Chapter 2.)

Information Structuring Guidelines

Information decomposition focuses on the creation of a list or outline of information objects. In information *structuring*, you work with that list or outline to create a diagram of information objects that shows how they are related. This is the **information structure diagram**. Before getting into a description of the diagram and an explanation of how it's created, it is important to stress once more that the process of Web presentation development does not take place across a neatly marked time line. In some cases, if the information to be put on the Web is fairly simple, designers may be able to go straight to the creation of an information structure diagram from a brief list of information objects; no outline is necessary. For more complex presentations, creating an outline, or even many outlines by user group, can be extremely helpful. In such cases the process of creating the information structure diagram may begin in tandem with the creation of the outline.

Creating a Web presentation is an organic process in which each activity, or step taken, likely has ramifications for some other part of the site. Thus it makes sense that the design of the information structure diagram would begin to suggest itself as the outline takes shape. For our purposes here, creation of the information structure diagram is discussed as distinct from decomposition, whereas in actual practice the processes are closely wedded. It is also important to realize that the outline and especially the information diagram will probably go through many drafts and revisions; this fact is evident in the Best Personalized Books case study.

Creating the Diagram

The information structure diagram is intended to guide upcoming stages of presentation development. In the diagram, information objects are drawn as rectangles, with the title of the information object in the rectangle. Lines drawn between the objects represent a network of associations, or linkages. Information structure diagrams are read top to bottom and left to right, and imply that there is a sequence to the information and the way it will be presented on the Web. So, at the lowest level of the international programs design, for instance, information about courses offered will be accessed through the "International Programs," "Timing," and "Location" information objects. (Refer to Figure 4-4.)

The information structure diagram also includes additional information about the information objects, such as how often each appears (known as **cardinality**) and how frequently its information might be subject to change (known as **volatility**). Actually, cardinality and volatility are likely to be noted first on one of the later versions of the outline created during decomposition.

As it is created, an outline might duplicate information in several places to show the information structure for each user group. In Web sites with hundreds of information objects, keeping all details at all levels of analysis obscures the process unnecessarily. Cardinality can eliminate the duplication of information objects, helping to streamline the outline and eventually the information structure diagram. This occurs by merging multiple occurrences of an object to show just *one* object. The object's cardinality, or number of occurrences, is marked on the outline (and the information structure diagram) for future use. The outline at the top of Figure 4-10 was derived from the resume in Figure 4-8. The numbers in parentheses indicate cardinality, or the number of times each information object occurs in the resume.

In addition to the number of occurrences of each object, the frequency of change, or **volatility**, is identified. This is an important piece of information because information objects that are highly volatile, that is, changing daily or even more frequently, need special attention so as to provide the level of information accuracy desired. A simple code can be devised to identify object volatility, such as A-annual, S-semiannual, M-monthly, W-weekly, D-daily, and so on. These codes would also appear in the outline in parentheses, following indications of cardinality (see the outline at the bottom of Figure 4-10). (Even nonvolatile information objects should be reviewed at least annually for accuracy. Continuing Web site success requires current information.) As you'll soon see, cardinality and volatility are recorded on the information structure diagram in a corner of the rectangle representing the information objects.

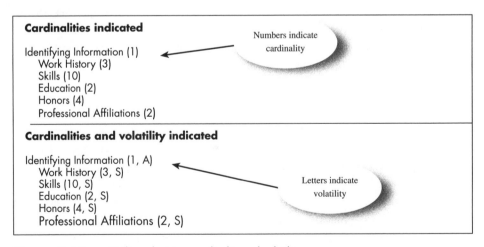

Figure 4-10   Outlines depicting cardinality and volatility

Figures 4-11a through c depict the evolution of an information structure diagram. In Figure 4-11a, a detailed resume is outlined. Its translation into a full information structure diagram is shown in Figure 4-11b. It is redrawn in summary format in Figure 4-11c, which makes it easier to see the structure of the diagram. This is in fact the preferred format, since in a large Web project (such as General Motors' thousands of pages) the details hinder design understanding rather than help it. In Figure 4-11c, each information object is shown once on the diagram. Each line between the boxes in such a summary diagram should represent a relationship between the information and some user or presenter need. (The basic types of relationships that can occur between information objects will be explained shortly.)

```
Identifying information (A)
Work history (S)
        Academic
                Baruch
                Georgia College
        Industry
                Merck
                Lambda Technology
                Ernst & Young
Skills (S)
        Hardware
                IBM
                Apple
                DEC
        Software
                Databases
                        IMS/DB
                        Access
                        SQL
                Telecommunications
                        IMS/DC
                        CICS
                        TCP/IP
        Languages
                Cobol
                Fortran
                C++
                Visual Basic
                IBM Assembler
Education (A)
        BS
        MBA
        Ph.D.
Honors (A)
        Teacher of the Year
        Researcher of the Year
        Grant from U.S. Army
        Grants from Baruch
Professional affiliations (A)
        ACM -- SIGMIS, SIGCHI, SIGOIS
        ICIS
                Program Committee
        IEEE -- Computer Society
Publications (M)
        Refereed* (20)
        Non-refereed* (20)
        Other (20)
Courses taught (15, M)

* Refereed publications are those which have been approved by a committee of one's professional peers;
nonrefereed publications have not gone through this process.
```

Figure 4-11a   Details of an academic's resume

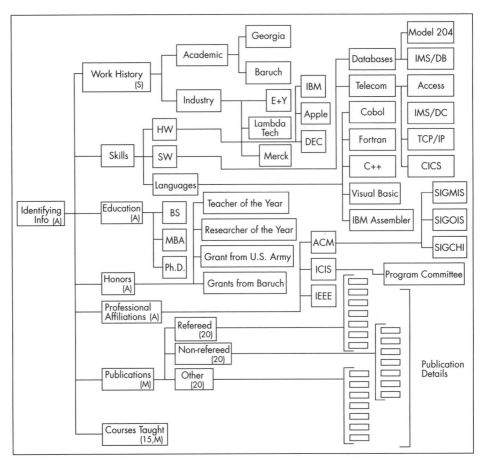

Figure 4-11b   Complete information structure diagram

The next step in diagramming the resume might be to analyze it from the perspective of potential users. How might an industry recruiter review the information? What about an academic recruiter? Figure 4-12a lists the likely information needs of the two recruiter types based on interviews with several of each. The diagram in Figure 4-12b (which builds on Figure 4-11c) uses broken lines so you can easily see the relationships between these needs as each user is likely to see them. These lines identify the *user* needs for information that are different from a traditional resume format. All of these needs should be accessible from the individual's home page resume. Unless this type of analysis takes place, it's easy to overlook them.

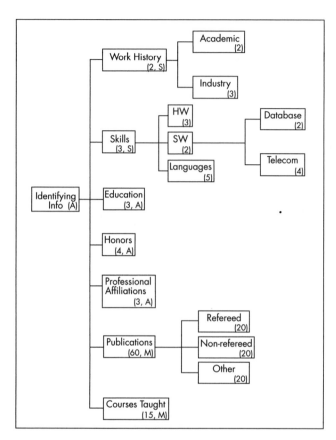

Figure 4-11c   Summary diagram

The challenge is to create pathways through the information that are meaningful to users. Essentially, you are creating a road map. It has a single starting point (which will be a Web home page) and then fans out into a network of major arteries (Web pages for primary information objects), secondary routes (with more detailed information objects), and return linkages (pathways back to different stops along the way), all designed with users' prior knowledge and interests in mind.

```
Outline
Industry recruiter needs
        Industry work history
        Education
        Skills
        Academic work history

Academic recruiter needs
        Academic work history
        Courses taught
        Refereed publications
        Professional affiliations
                Offices
        Languages
```

Figure 4-12a   Information needs of different recruiters

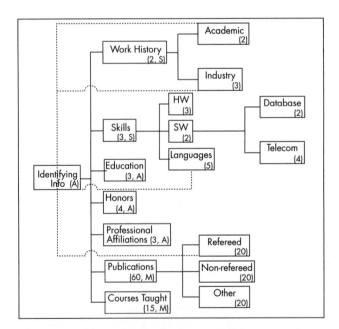

Figure 4-12b   Relationships between information needs

Another way to visualize the information structure is in terms of a hierarchical chart or tree diagram, like one you might use to trace your family tree or create an organization chart. The difference is that in a Web hierarchy, a single information object may have many relationships, and the relationships are not restricted to a hierarchical arrangement.

Building Relationships Between Information Objects

Several types of relationships can exist between information objects, each depending on the nature of the objects being connected. The three types discussed here are general-specific (gen-spec), is-a, and associative. The first two types, gen-spec and is-a, relate to information content and stem more from the presenter's perspective on the Web site. The third type, associative relationships, stem more from the user's perspective. They add value for users by completing threads and providing closure on some activity or information.

As explained in Chapter 1, a **thread** is a sequence of relationships that defines a path through a set of pages. Recall the notion of **closure**, mentioned in Chapter 3, by which each thread provides a complete information experience for the user. Closure is what the user should find at the end of each thread. It means that all or at least part of the user's need to travel down that particular path has been satisfied. Closure can come in the form of simple enjoyment of the Web site, an opportunity to make a request for information, or success in obtaining information.

The first information-relationship type, **general-to-specific**, or **gen-spec**, identifies, logically enough, information that moves from the general to the specific. One example of the gen-spec relationship in information is, as you may recall from high school science, the classification of the animal world. Its movement from kingdom to phylum to class to order, family, genus, and species is a movement from general to specific. Another example is the course catalog described earlier in the chapter, which progressed from a set of general headings giving program titles to detailed information about each particular course in the program. Text-based information objects often have a gen-spec relationship.

A second type of relationship information objects may share, the **is-a relationship**, occurs when an information object retains the basic identity of its parent object while still being unique unto itself. For instance, C++ *is-a* specific instance of a programming skill. It is one skill among many that a professional programmer might have. Here *programming skills* represent the parent object; C++ is still like its parent object in being a skill, but it is also unique to itself because it can be distinguished from all other programming skills. Another example can be seen in General Motors, or any other car and truck maker. GM manufactures vehicles, of which cars and trucks are examples. Both have *is-a* relationships. That is, a car *is a* vehicle. Similarly, a Chevrolet *is a* car. And a Corvette *is a* Chevrolet.

Associative relationships, a third type of relationship between information objects, are most meaningful to users. To develop associative relationships between information objects, designers and stewards examine each group of users separately to determine what information the group might want to follow through the presentation. For instance, a customer checking order status might next want to change an order. If that service is not available in the Web presentation, the customer might want to send an e-mail or file an information request. Information objects that perform such tasks are linked to create the association. The goal in defining associative relationships is to provide closure. The broken lines added to Figure 4-12b indicate recruiters' information needs and are an example of associative relationships.

Relationships of interest to the presenter—gen-spec and is-a—are usually represented in the first lines drawn on the information structure diagram. Relationships that add value for users (associative relationships) follow. The value-added relationships lengthen the threads and increase crossover of threads between objects representing different areas of the business or organizations. Associative relationships can be drawn as either solid lines or as dotted lines, as they are in Figure 4-12b. Dotted lines are useful for tracking associations.

The Object Relationship Matrix

In complex presentations it can be useful to develop an **object relationship matrix** as part of (or preceding the process of) creating an information structure diagram. The purpose of the matrix is to show all of the linkages from one information object to another as a means of showing the extent of interconnectedness. An object relationship matrix facilitates linkage evaluation by summarizing linkage coverage over all objects.

In this matrix, which is set up like a spreadsheet, each information object is listed across the top and again down the left side of the paper or screen. Each cell of the matrix, or row/column intersection, contains a mark if the two objects are related, and is left empty if they are not related.

Figure 4-13 shows an object relationship matrix for the resume information in Figure 4-11. Notice that each column and each row must have at least one entry, otherwise, an orphan object (one with no relationship to any other, and so with no link to any other) would exist. When marking relationships between objects, it's important to mark each relationship *only once*. Figure 4-14 shows a close-up of a corner of the matrix. Notice that there's an X at the intersection of the work history row and the ID information column, indicating there's a relationship between the two. Also notice that there is *not* another X at the intersection of the ID information *row* and the work history *column* because that would be duplicating information. Each relationship should be recorded in the matrix only once.

If more than 50% of the cells in any single column or row are marked, there's a possibility that the object represented is a **critical linking object**, one that is required for users to understand the lower-level information. Such an object requires careful text composition (discussed in Chapter 5) and design. Of course, such a high rate of marking also may simply mean that the object has too many relationships and that the number of relationships should be reduced.

In general, if under 10% of possible linkages are used, the user groups may not be fully served. The number of linkages possible is the number of information objects less one. For example, if there are 16 information objects, each can have 1 to 15 relationships. The percentage of relationships is the number of linkages identified divided by the number of possible relationships. Also in general, if more than 80% of possible linkages are used, the site is probably mapped too heavily and is confusing. The number of linkages should be reduced.

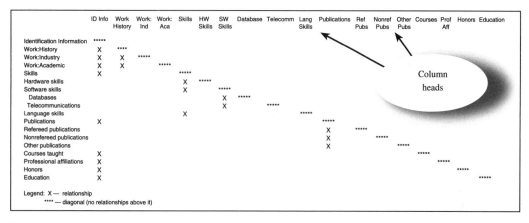

Figure 4-13   The object relationship matrix

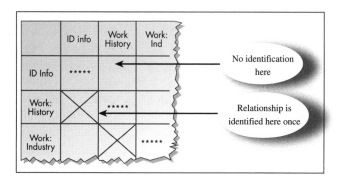

Figure 4-14   Marking relationships

One rule of thumb is to limit objects to between one and five relationships (the lower end of the 7 ± 2 rule). Beyond that, users have increasing difficulty identifying any relationship pattern. They cannot decipher the direction of the threads through the pages and often get lost. The optimal number of connections, if there is such a thing, remains an area of research.

Testing Different Linkage Arrangements

Before finalizing the information structure, it is important to try out different arrangements of information objects and to test different paths, or threads, through the information. Noted Web designers Bonnie Wyper and Stephen Greco, who designed a nutrition information site called Diet Central, summarize their work on the site during the information structuring phase as follows: "To begin creating a . . . design, we mapped and remapped the information into an architecture we thought was consistent with the way people would want to access it. . . . We thought out paths through the information [and] considered alternate paths."[2]

Testing guards against creating a Web site that does not adequately meet user and presenter needs. One way to test information structure is to bring together likely Web site users in focus groups. Each group can try out linkages that have been incorporated into the structure specifically for users like themselves. Company employees who are not involved in the Web presentation development can also be used.

Testing different threads is simplified by using the 3x5 card method of defining information objects. Once the information objects are defined, the cards are placed on a surface that allows you to draw (and erase and then redraw) lines between them. Several trial arrangements of the cards and the lines between

GO to...

http://www.dietcentral.com
the Diet Central Web site that Wyper and Greco developed by means of thorough decomposition and analysis of their information domain.

them might be necessary to develop one that provides closure on all threads for all intended user groups. When the desired structure is found, the diagram is created either on paper or in an automated drawing tool (such as Visio). Paper-and-pencil drawings are less formal and are useful for small projects whose contents are unlikely to change. Automated drawings work well with large or highly volatile projects because it's easier to manipulate the information (and to print out clean copies).

Web Design in the Real World

Best Personalized Books

Best's business information structure is shown in Figure 4-15. The structure identifies information relating to the business: marketing, company history, current news, and order processing. These topics are typical of most companies.

Sue took the outline of the information structure, adding user linkages as Jack directed, and created an initial information structure diagram, shown in Figure 4-16.

(Indications of cardinality and volatility have been left out to simplify reading of figures.) As Jack envisioned, potential licensees got a subset of the information available to current licensees. As designers, Sue and Dick were unhappy with the diagram because of the duplication of information in the existing and potential licensees' sets of information and threads. Sue suggested changes to reduce the duplication of information and create

2. Bonnie Wyper and Stephen Greco, "Design Online," *Communication Arts*, May/June, 1997, 24.

```
Company information
                Introductory information
                Background & history (includes growth statistics)
                Awards
                Distinctive competency — unique patented technology, growing product lines
                        with licensing arrangements with Disney, etc.
                Emphasis on quality
                Multilingual products
                4 reasons why Best is best
        Testimonials of successful licensees
        The process of creating a book (what a licensee does)
        Languages of books
        Product samples
        Buy a book — form
                Customer identifying information
                Item type
                Custom personalization information form
        Become a licensee
                Computer requirements
                Licensing procedure
                The process of creating a book (what a licensee does)
                Best company support
        Marketing support
                Marketing support products
                Selling techniques
        Existing licensee support
                Marketing support
                        Marketing support products
                        Selling techniques
                Product samples
                Purchasing — form for product purchase
                        Security information
                        Purchase form (automatically displays licensee
                                name/address information and any pre-arranged
                                financing information)
```

Figure 4-15
Best information outline

a single set of pages for certain kinds of information—for example, marketing information—for both licensees and nonlicensees. The most important changes were:

- narrower definition of the secure area of information accessible to current licensees only

- consolidation of all duplicated threads

- removal of the need for licensees to provide security information as they enter the site, allowing for single storage of information accessible by licensees and the general public

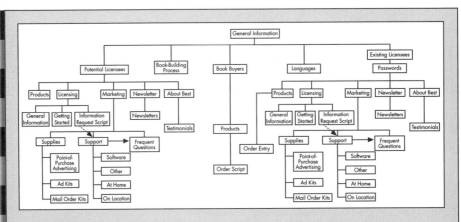

Figure 4-16
Best initial information structure

The effect of these changes was to produce the diagram in Figure 4-17. This diagram was less complex and appeared to make business sense. When Wendy and Jack reviewed the diagram, it looked less cluttered, but they still had difficulty visualizing what the pages and links would look like. This is a typical reaction at this stage. Sue and Dick suggested that the team review the threads and later, after completing the information structure diagram, build a prototype. Looking at a prototype, Wendy and Jack would be able to see their pages and the links and make comments on an actual Web presentation. The prototype would be on the computer, but not connected to the Internet. At this stage, it would be text only, but it would show which information objects would be on which pages and would provide linkages between pages.

Before building the prototype, Sue and Dick reviewed the actions each user group would need to take to navigate the pages. The information at the top of the hierarchy was either placed directly on the Best home page or made accessible through a link on the home page. For instance, most home pages are an index to the rest of the site. In addition, identifying information is needed to convert surfers to users. In Best's case, both book buyers and potential licensees were expected to want to see products and the book-building process. So both of those topics were elevated to the Best home page.

Within the Best information structure, the is-a relationship is most evident in the individual product descriptions. For example, a Christmas story book *is-an* example of a product. Each individual edition of the Best newsletter *is-an* example of the newsletter as a collective information object.

Gen-spec relationships are most evident in the marketing information. Marketing

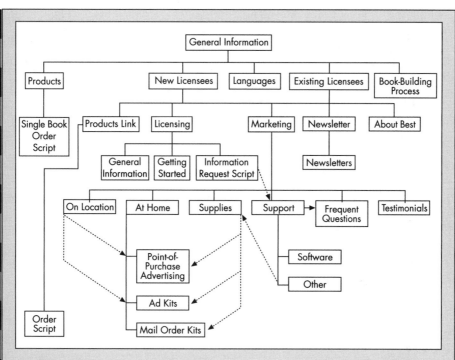

Figure 4-17
Best revised information structure

support included software, supplies, and phone assistance. The supplies further decomposed into support products for location sales, mail order, and advertising kits. Access to the supplies information was desired for both potential and current licensees, who would want to see what was available and get an idea of the support, so those links were created.

A discussion was held about the personal characteristics of the licensees and their ability to relate to terms such as "marketing support." Licensees were predominantly selling Best products as a part-time business and were not familiar with "corporate"

terminology. Wendy and Jack wanted to make sure the Web site contained no terms that the general public would not understand. They didn't want to alienate or confuse their users. Jack and Wendy were also concerned about users' ability to navigate the site, and suggested limiting the number of information hierarchy levels to three or four to facilitate navigation.

This discussion gave the designers a better understanding of the users. It was revisited during the process of deciding on the actual wording of Web text (see Chapter 5). This discussion also drove the definition of the associative relationships.

Sue and Dick were now able to define the mental maps of the licensees and surmise how they would want to view the information. Sue and Dick elevated the location sales, home sales, and supplies information objects to make them accessible both from the higher-level marketing information in the information structure diagram (see Figure 4-18) and from their original location as licensee support.

Further discussion about how support would be provided when licensees had questions led to the development of a new information object for a support request. A support request is a request from a licensee who wants to find the best way of selling a book or performing part of the book creation process. These requests usually come through the toll-free telephone line but are also received from other countries by mail. Once the Web site was online, support requests could also be entered through the Web site and e-mailed directly to the Best Webmaster. (**Webmaster** is a general title given to a Web site's e-mail account; in reality, Mike Heischman was the Best Webmaster and the e-mail was directed to him.) The support request information object was added to the general support list of information.

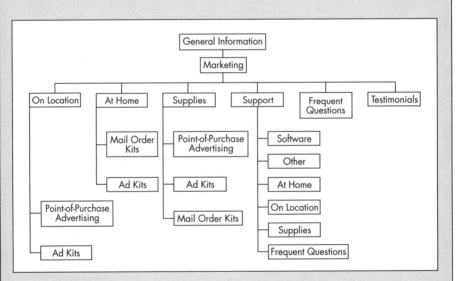

Figure 4-18
Marketing information structure

Similar discussions were held for all of the information objects in the diagram. The team stopped referring to them as "information objects" and started talking about them as both "boxes on the page"—meaning on the information structure diagram—and as "Web pages." This shift occurred sometime during the marketing discussion and signaled a shift of understanding for everyone that each "box" on the diagram represented one or more "pages" on the Web site. It was a subtle clue that both Wendy and Jack had reached a level of understanding that allowed them to visualize "pages," even though they couldn't say what was on them at that point.

This shift in Wendy and Jack's thinking would also make it easier for them to imagine and discuss how potential users might think about the site and the company instead of focusing on what they (the presenters) think. The user now became the focus of all conversations, and the design was user-centered at this point. From the designers' experience, this was a rapid transition, demonstrating the depth of the Kalishers' empathy for their targeted user groups. The conversations moved along more rapidly and toward details of page design in almost every discussion.

The other significant discussion related to the decisions about current licensee activities. Notice that in Figure 4-19 the only information warranting secured access (entered through the order security check page) is order information and its two components—product information (a hyperlink) and the order script page. The difference in the secured product information (as compared with unsecured product information) was the addition of quantity and price for book covers, paper stock, and so on.

The group decided that the licensees were likely to enter their secured area immediately and would like access to other information without moving in and out of the secured area. The licensees were likely to have support requests or questions about doing business, or want to know the latest company news. Therefore, links were added to allow access to the marketing support request page, to frequently asked questions, and to the newsletter. Ultimately, the team decided to allow access to all unsecured pages from the secured part of the site, but entry (and reentry) to the secured area would require use of a password.

The final information structure diagram (see Figure 4-19) shows the links added to make Web presentation navigation more intuitive for the user and to lead each group of users to closure on activities they were likely to pursue.

To check the coverage of linkages between information objects, Sue and Dick developed an initial object relationship

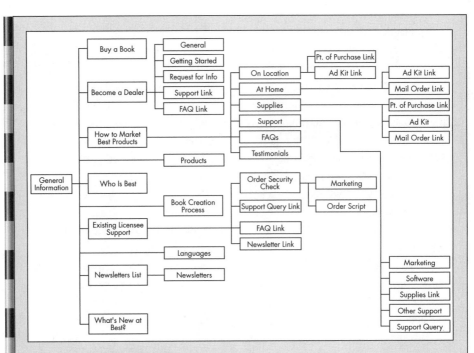

Figure 4-19
Final information structure diagram

matrix for Best (see Figure 4-20). The percentage of possible linkages fell below 10%, so they conducted another review of the linkages. Each user group's needs were shown to be filled, and the links Jack and Wendy thought to be important to their business were complete and accurate. The team decided to review the issue again after the prototype was available for review.

The information relationship matrix shows a low number of linkages, but the team found them adequate to move on to the next phase of Web development. Once the decision to allow individuals to purchase a book via the Internet had been reached, there was no further discussion of the issue until the team discussed the specifics of Web pages. This issue, and those relating to potential licensee capabilities, did not recur until the text analysis phase, which is the subject of Chapter 5.

Figure 4-20
Best object relationship matrix

	Home Page	Book making process	15 Languages	7 Product Lines	Buy a Book	What's new at Best?	Become dealer	Who is Best?	Marketing Best products	Existing licensee support	On location	Best supplies	FAQs	At home	Best Support	Testimonials	Order Form	Newsletter list	Newsletter 1...n	Dealer information	Dealer inquiry	Email
Home Page	----																					
Book making process	G/R	----																				
15 Languages	G/R		----																			
7 Product Lines	G/R			----																		
Buy a Book	G/R			G/R	----																	
What's new at Best?	G/R					----																
Become dealer	G/R						----															
Who is Best?	G/R		G/					----														
Marketing Best products	G/R								----													
Existing licensee support	/R								G/R	----												
On location	/R								G/R		----											
Best supplies	/R								G/R			----										
FAQs	/R								G/R				----									
At home	/R								G/R					----								
Best Support	/R								G/R						----							
Testimonials	/R					G/R			G/R							----						
Order Form	/R			G/R													----					
Newsletter list	/R					G/R												----				
Newsletter 1...n	/R																	G/R	----			
Dealer information	/R						G/R													----		
Dealer inquiry	/R						G/R													G/R	----	
Email	G/R	G/R	G/R	G/R	G/R	G/R	G/R	G/R	G/R	G/R	G/R	G/R	G/R	G/R	G/R	G/R	G/R	G/R	G/R	G/R	G/R	----

Summary

The goal of information decomposition is to break down information into specific information objects, creating a description that identifies each object's origin for the Web presentation. The description can be a list, outline, 3x5 card, or database entry. For any given origin, there should be a single entry for each object even though the information may be present in several forms or media. Type of media is not considered at this point except to define a source of information. The result of information decomposition documents information objects, each carefully named to identify like objects of multiple origins with the same name, and all others as unique objects with different names.

The information structuring step is important because the information structure diagram determines what each Web page will communicate and the extent to which the needs of users will be met. The step is accomplished by three activities:

1. Define relationships between information objects beyond those related to an object's origin.

2. Develop alternative relationship structures to define the threads of user interest.

3. Choose the information object structure that becomes the blueprint for Web presentation development.

Threads link information objects together to meet users' needs and define business relationships.

Relationships can be identified by examining a specific information object and its immediate parent object. Relationships can show is-a, gen-spec, and associative types of information. Is-a relationships identify a child-object that is an example or instance of its parent object. Gen-spec objects are specific, more detailed information about a general parent object. Associative objects are objects that relate because the relationship has meaning to either the business or to expected users.

A matrix of information object relationships can be developed to evaluate and document linkages between objects.

R e v i e w   Q u e s t i o n s

1. Why is it necessary to decompose a body of information before designing a successful Web presentation?

2. What is the relationship between atomic information objects and chunks?

3. What is the value of knowing the source of an information object?

4. What is the benefit to the designer in developing an information structure diagram? What is the benefit to the presenting company?

5. How can you "play" with different structural arrangements? Why would you want to do that?

6. What is meant by the volatility of an information object? Why is volatility important? What are the implications of highly volatile information objects, such as stock prices, for Web presentation design?

7. Define the gen-spec, is-a, and associative information relationship. In a Web site on baking bread, what relationship describes the link between baking time and an automatic timer that can be purchased from the sponsor of the site? Between an instruction to knead the bread and a description of how to do it? Between the ingredient "flour" and a list of types of flour?

8. Describe the relationship between a user's mental map and the threads defined during information structuring.

P r o j e c t s

1. Find a Web site that presents a complex body of audio information (an example is http://www.audionet.com). Decompose the information and develop an information structure diagram of it. Identify and discuss the significant information structure decisions that the designers and information stewards had to make. Can you tell what assumptions they made about groups of users from the structure?

2. Look at three different university catalogues from schools that have Web sites (to find schools, go to http://www.edunet.com/uni-usa.html). Compare and contrast the Web information to the printed matter. What are the similarities and differences in information organization? Which school does the best job of structuring its information in both locations? Is the school that structured printed information best also the best on the Web? Why or why not?

C a s e   P r o j e c t

1. From all of the sources you've gathered for your Web presentation, prepare a set of specific information objects. Develop an outline of the information that identifies each object's origin. Also, for objects that come in multiples, identify the number of each that you will have. You may also want to record each information object on individual 3x5 index cards or enter them into a database.

2. Develop an information structure diagram for your project. First, include only the gen-spec and is-a relationships that flow from the business relationships between the objects.

3. Analyze each group of users' expected use of the information objects. The goal is to define associative relationships. Move the index cards around in different configurations (or with different relationship lines between them) to arrive at the most complete information structure. Use a checklist to ensure that you have discussed all expected uses for each thread by each group of users.

4. When you have discussed all users' threads, look at the "whole" diagram, analyzing any patterns of objects/relationships to consolidate duplications or remove artificial hierarchy that might inhibit Web presentation use. Keep this information for use in the coming chapter exercises.

F u r t h e r   R e a d i n g

- Landrow, George P. *Hypertext: The Convergence of Contemporary Critical Theory and Technology.* Baltimore: Johns Hopkins University Press, 1992.

- Marcus, Aaron. *Graphic Design for Electronic Documents and User Interfaces.* New York: ACM Press, 1991.

- Mok, Clement. *Designing Business: Multiple Media, Multiple Disciplines.* San Jose, Calif.: Adobe Press, 1996.

- Sano, Darrell. *Designing Large-Scale Web Sites: A Visual Design Methodology.* New York: John Wiley & Sons, 1997.

- Tufte, Edward R. *Envisioning Information.* Cheshire, Conn.: Graphics Press, 1990.

- Wyper, Bonnie, and Stephen Greco. "Design Online." *Communication Arts*, May/June, 1997, 23-28.

DESIGN METHODS

Part 3

DESIGN METHODS

The chapters in this part of the book describe the hands-on activities involved in the Web presentation design phase. Each process involved—designing text (Chapter 5), designing hyperlinks (Chapter 6), and designing multimedia (Chapter 7)—basically consists of two steps: analysis and composition. For the purposes of this book, **analysis** refers to the act of identifying the available options (as applied to text, hyperlinks, and multimedia), and **composition** refers to selecting from and organizing or implementing those options. Thus, the Web presentation design phase progresses something like this:

1. Establish the content and the location of each information object through text analysis and composition.

2. Identify targets for and implement hyperlinks.

3. Identify options for and implement multimedia.

4. Test and revise all of the above as necessary.

The fourth step, test and revise, is important because in developing the design the Web presentation team actually cycles through each of the above activities many times. Here as elsewhere in the book, the appearance of discrete steps is just that: an appearance. In actual Web development the steps overlap and may occur simultaneously.

5

Text Analysis and Composition

In This Chapter You Will Learn To:

- Identify the goals of writing text for Web presentations
- Create text that contributes to affectiveness, effectiveness, and navigational efficiency
- Apply the four principles of information object arrangement
- Apply five methods of grouping information
- Apply the principles of color design
- Make appropriate use of maps, menus, and frames in Web page formatting

Web Design in the Real World

Best Personalized Books

Once the information structure diagram was complete, Sue and Dick were ready to use it to begin to create the text portion of the Best Web presentation. During this critical portion of the Web design process, the content and position of all text on all Web pages would be decided.

Overview: Text Analysis and Composition

The text portion of a Web presentation conveys the presentation's key message. For this reason, almost every word of it must be scrutinized. **Text analysis** is the development of the prose statements that most clearly convey the intended message of each information object contained in the information structure diagram. (If the information object is not text, the underlying idea of the object is described in a few words.)

During **text composition**, all of the objects with complete text are arranged and rearranged, grouped and regrouped, until the placement is found that best serves the interests of the site—in other words, the placement that best achieves the principles of effectiveness, affectiveness, and navigational efficiency.

Key Roles

Information stewards are very active during text analysis. They are responsible for making sure the text associated with each information object is accurate and complete. While designers may help to evaluate the text and sometimes contribute to writing, this aspect of Web presentation design normally belongs to information stewards. Depending on the importance of the Web pages to the organization, professional writers might be engaged as consultants to participate in this activity. Final approval of the text should be obtained widely within the presenting organization, including the owner(s), stewards, and the legal and public relations departments. Review by other departments may also be desired depending on the page contents. It is especially important to get approval from managers or representatives whose departments have actually contributed to the Web presentation.

Text composition is largely the job of the designer; skills in text and graphic design are crucial to this part of the Web design process. Information stewards are primarily responsible for evaluating text once it has been composed.

Text Analysis Guidelines

The first step in text analysis is to return to the sources of the information objects in the information diagram. Each source—brochure, newsletter, product, etc.—should be carefully reviewed and decomposed into its constituent parts, whatever they may be—a message, a piece of data, an idea.

After text decomposition, each word and idea is examined for its relevance to the information object's message. If it is not relevant, it is discarded. If it is relevant, it is added to the list of ideas to be conveyed. When this analysis is complete for a single information object, the next step, writing, can begin. During the writing phase, each object's main idea is identified. Then, a sentence that conveys that idea is written. If there are several supporting ideas, one introductory sentence plus one sentence for each different supporting idea is written. If there is more than one main idea, the information object itself needs more decomposition. In this case, you would recycle back through the activities in Chapter 4.

Once written, the information objects are edited, with a focus on enhancing their effective and affective attributes and on maintaining their distinct identities. Several keywords describing each information object should be identified for use in creating hyperlink text. (Creation of hyperlink text is discussed in the next chapter.)

Writing for Effect and Affect

Recall that *effectiveness* is the extent to which the information conveyed is accurate and complete. To judge the effectiveness of the text, ask such questions as: What is the central thought of each sentence? Does each sentence convey the desired meaning? Does it fit well into the context in which it will be viewed? Does it add value for the user, especially the first-time user? If the answer to any of these questions is no, additional rewriting and editing are probably needed. Alternatives are to change, delete, or add text or numerical information.

Ambiguity usually does not make for effectiveness. Occasionally an ambiguous or cryptic statement can be captivating, but it usually results in misinterpretation and the loss of a potential user. For example, an organization may be described as "well established" for several different reasons: because it has been in business a long time, because it has a large, growing customer base, or simply because it has not gone out of business. This ambiguity may be useful if the organization has something it wants to disguise, say its size or age. Ambiguous statements are most often unconvincing when the organization is making the statement as the basis for a sale. In that case (and probably most others), specifics are more persuasive, as in "the company has been in business ten years" or "the company has more than 1,000 satisfied customers."

All of the writing goals summarized in Figure 5-1 are concerned with the effectiveness of Web page content. The goals are listed in order of importance, with completeness and accuracy being the most important.

Writing Goal	Definition
Complete or comprehensive	The text covers all aspects of the idea to be communicated.
Accurate or labeled with accuracy level	The text is factually correct. If there is speculative information, it is labeled as such.
Easy to read	The text uses short, uncomplicated sentence structure and is written at a high school level.
Clear	The text has a single meaning and interpretation.
Useful to at least one defined audience	The text specifically provides information, function, or access to information that a steward-defined user wants.
Concise	The text is short, with no extra words.

Figure 5-1   Writing goals

Meeting the writing goals expressed in Figure 5-1 can be a difficult task. Sometimes trade-offs must be made. For example, very technical texts, such as product specifications, demand a level of accuracy and completeness that may be impossible to achieve without sacrificing some readability. But easy reading is not what the audience for such material will be looking for.

Still, an attempt should be made at the outset to reach for each of the goals listed in Figure 5-1. Writers should review and rewrite several versions of text for each information object to ensure that all goals have been considered.

Sometimes the drive for completeness and clarity in achieving writing goals can uncover political issues or deep-seated ambiguities that have been in the organization for some time. For instance, an insurance company might find that the term "policyholder" has many legitimate definitions depending on its use by the organization's various departments. Who then should have the authority to decide how "a policyholder" will be defined on the Web site? Once information stewards agree on the wording of all text, a group of people who are not involved in Web development (but who are from the department responsible for the information) should critique it. Then several potential users who are not in the organization should be gathered in a focus group to critique it. One approach is to ask those reviewing the text to rate it on all of the criteria listed in Figure 5-1. Another is to ask reviewers to describe the goals, audience, and meaning they infer from the text; that is, what does it suggest to them? Based on the evaluations and comments received, the text should be revised.

The *affectiveness* of a presentation—its ability to speak to the user on an emotional level—is very much influenced by tone. Active voice, for example, is generally more engaging than passive voice. To make a point, give a direction or an instruction, or provide a strong argument, use active voice. (Examples: "You will receive a discount." "ABC Company endorses this policy.") Passive voice gives the impression of reaction rather than action. (Examples: "A discount will be received." "This policy is endorsed by ABC Company.") Tone also can convey intensity, attitude, and emotion. A sales-oriented tone may be appropriate for an intense marketing presentation, but not for a literary magazine.

GO to...

http://www.ge.com
where General Electric uses a direct, positive, active approach to describe the options available on its Web site.

Writing for Navigational Efficiency

After each information object is written for the Web, key words that express the essential idea of the information object are identified and annotated (using techniques described below under "Text Composition Guidelines"). When page locations for all information objects are initially determined, these words are then analyzed collectively to determine the Web page headings and hyperlink identifiers.

For the home page, for instance, decisions are made about what essential words will be used to identify or describe the company, to convince a surfer that the site is worth exploring, and to convey a concise and accurate impression of the Web site contents. Lower-level pages each require one or more levels of header and one or more hyperlinks to other information, pages, or sites; phrases must be developed for all of these items. It can be difficult to decide on phrasing, especially for the home page. Because the words there represent the entire company to a Web surfer, they must be chosen carefully. To turn surfers into users, phrasing must be crisp and clear, meaningful to all viewers, and interesting. These are not small goals.

Reevaluating the Text

Before completing text analysis, reevaluate the information objects as a group. Because information object relationships can be altered, created, or even lost during rewriting, it's important to review the information structure (the organization of the objects in relation to each other) to make sure it still makes sense. Further changes to the text or to the structure may be necessary. The result of text analysis should be a prose description of each information object to be included in the presentation.

Text Composition Guidelines

Once written, the text needs to be **composed**—that is, the text for each information object is arranged in an aesthetically and artistically pleasing relationship with every other information object. Text composition is a critical step in developing Web presentations. It consists of three basic building blocks : layout, typography, and color.

Layout refers to the placement of text (and all other kinds of media) on the Web page. Where will each text object be positioned on each page or screen? How wide and long will the columns be? How much space will be placed between lines of text? What alignment will be used—left, right, center? Will the page be text only, or will it use more advanced designs such as multiple columns, graphical maps, or frames? All of these questions need to be answered in deciding on layout.

Typography refers to typeface, type style, and type size. **Typeface** refers to the design of the type. One typeface often used in business today is Times Roman. Another is Helvetica. Both have a simple appearance and are easy to read. There are hundreds of other typefaces to choose from, each of which will bring a different expressive quality to the text. Choice of typeface contributes considerably to the affectiveness of a Web site.

Certain **type styles** can be applied to any typeface. Examples are *italic* and **bold**, which are used to highlight selected text, and roman, or regular, type, which is what you are reading right now.

Type size, which is measured in points rather than inches or centimeters (there are 72 points in an inch), can vary greatly and should be used sensibly as well as creatively. It's always important to put basic reading text in a size (and face and style) that makes for comfortable reading. You don't want to lose a potential user simply because he or she finds the type too small to read. The smallest recommended type size for use on screen is 8 points. (The text you're reading now was set in 10-point type.) And 8-point type should be used only for menu entries, not for lines or paragraphs of text. The largest practical type size is whatever can be fit into a single line. The bulk of screen text should be between 12 and 18 points—big enough to read, small enough for a sensible onscreen fit.

Color is a vital part of Web presentations, particularly as it is applied to hyperlinks. But color also contributes to legibility (a dark color type on a light color background will be easy to read, a light color on a light color will not) and to mood and tone, all of which contribute to a site's affectiveness. In composing text information objects, layout is performed first, followed by decisions on typography and color, which are made simultaneously.

Working with these three building blocks, you can (and should) use a number of different techniques to actually compose your text. Five primary approaches are presented here: arrangement, grouping, storyboarding, page format, and evaluation. An explanation of these approaches follows. One thing to keep in mind throughout this process of Web design, however, is the user—you want the text to be brief enough, informative enough, and complete enough to make the user want to keep viewing the presentation. Also bear in mind that many iterations of text composition are not unusual.

Text Arrangement

Four key principles drive the arrangement of information objects on a page: proximity, alignment, contrast, and repetition.

Proximity refers to the practice of placing information objects that contain similar or related information near each other. One criterion for proximity might be volatility. For instance, Web newspapers provide information at several levels of volatility: highly volatile news such as a kidnapping in progress, less volatile news such as sports scores, and selectively volatile news such as movie reviews. Sports sites that follow games in progress can also have different levels of volatility. For example, baseball scores are updated when a score changes, but game schedules only change annually. The reason to arrange volatile objects by proximity is to minimize the number of pages that need updating when highly volatile information objects change.

Another criterion for proximity is relationships between information objects. For instance, on a résumé, an individual might list several educational degrees, several past jobs, many skills, and so on. The information could be ordered according to time, information object type, importance to the individual, and so on. By custom, we normally group information according to its type, or principal subject matter. This means that skills would be listed together, as would all jobs and all educational degrees. Much of proximity grouping is based on making common sense.

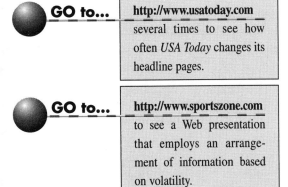

GO to... **http://www.usatoday.com** several times to see how often *USA Today* changes its headline pages.

GO to... **http://www.sportszone.com** to see a Web presentation that employs an arrangement of information based on volatility.

Alignment is the positioning of page elements relative to the edges of the page. Alignment can be left, right, or centered (see Figure 5-2 for examples of each). Alignment should be consistently applied throughout the pages. Left alignment is the most common, with unaligned, or ragged, right margins. Center alignment is not recommended for large blocks of text because both sides (left and right) have a ragged edge, which makes it difficult to read. However, centering of important text, such as titles and headers on an otherwise left-aligned page, draws attention to key information. Right alignment has the strongest affect because we are not used to seeing it. Right alignment also makes long passages difficult to read.

Other recommendations on alignment are to use multiple columns for long text passages, just as magazines and reference books often do. A two- or three-column format (see Figure 5-2) can accommodate more words per page than single-column text. This is partly because multiple columns make it possible to use more of the space available on the page—that is, the left and right margins can be narrower, thereby making room for more text. The shorter reading line in multiple-column text also makes it possible to use a smaller type size—that is, the shorter line is easier to read.[1] Generally, material on a Web page should be presented within the confines of the default screen display, which is approximately 6x4 inches. Wide single-column text is especially at a disadvantage if it extends beyond this area. Scrolling can become both awkward and time-consuming, increasing the risk of losing the viewer.

Contrast is the use of different design elements to highlight the differences between things. For instance, contrast can be used to identify different levels of information, distinguishing a heading from a subheading or more detailed text. One way to achieve contrast is through choice of typeface, style, and size. In general, headings are distinguished from other levels of text by use of larger type size, bolder type style, or a different typeface. As shown in the bottom box in Figure 5-3, headings might be presented in a 24-point, sans serif type such as Arial Black, while the detailed information might be presented in a 12-point, serif type such as Garamond. (The word "serif" refers to the short, light lines projected off the tops and bottoms of letters in a typeface like Garamond. In a typeface such as Arial, the letters are completely squared off. See Figure 5-3.) The contrast between serif and sans serif typefaces is used to help distinguish headers from the basic narrative text. Serif fonts are a good choice for material appearing in a smaller type size or for lengthy text, because they are easier to read.

---

1. *The Chicago Manual of Style,* 14th ed. (Chicago: University of Chicago Press, 1993), 769.

Building a home?

Let our experience transform your ideas into reality.

Your local Timberglen independent representative is key -- a specialist in the building industry drawing upon our resources as an award winning, national company with over 20 years' experience in designing and crafting fine post and beam homes.

Your Timberglen rep's first responsibility is to listen. To hear about what you expect from your new home -- details and finishes you like, color schemes that please you, and anything else that defines your taste and style.

Traditional — left-aligned

Building a home?

Let our
experience
transform
your ideas
into reality.

Your local Timberglen independent representative
is key -- a specialist in the building industry
drawing upon our resources as an
award winning, national company
with over 20 years' experience in
designing and crafting fine post and beam homes.

Your Timberglen rep's first responsibility is to
listen. To hear about what
you expect from your new home --
details and finishes you like,
color schemes that please you, and
anything else that defines your taste and style.

Nontraditional — right-aligned

Building a home?

Let our experience transform your ideas into reality.

Your local Timberglen independent representative is key -- a
specialist in the building industry drawing upon our resources as
an award winning, national company with over 20 years'
experience in
designing and crafting fine post and beam homes.

Your Timberglen rep's first responsibility is to listen. To hear
about what you expect from your new home -- details and finishes
you like, color schemes that please you, and anything else that
defines your taste and style.

Nontraditional — centered

Building a home?

Let our experience
transform your ideas
into reality.

Your local Timberglen
independent
representative is key --
a specialist in the
building industry
drawing upon our
resources as an award
winning, national
company with over 20
years' experience in

designing and crafting
fine post and beam
homes.

Your Timberglen rep's
first responsibility is to
listen. To hear about
what you expect from
your new home --
details and finishes you
like, color schemes that
please you, and
anything else that
defines your taste
and style.

Two-column format

Figure 5-2 Text alignment

Before

If you are planning to build the home of your dreams, you'll get all the help you need to build the home you want. Your local Timberglen independent representative is the key. He or she is a specialist in the building industry and draws upon our vast resources as an award-winning, national company with over 20 years' experience in designing and crafting fine post and beam homes. Your Timberglen independent representative's first responsibility is to listen. To hear about what you expect from your new home. He or she will take notes on details and finishes you like, color schemes that please you, and anything else that defines your taste and style.

After

Figure 5-3 Contrast and alignment

Contrast can also help to identify a **focal point**, that is, a place on the Web page to which you want the viewer's eyes to be drawn. The focal point might consist of text, graphic, icon, or other design elements and should be designed to contrast with the surrounding area of the presentation so it naturally captures the viewer's attention. In general, the focal point is anything large enough and different enough from the rest of the surrounding text to capture attention. Size is a large component of focal point. Large text size, a large graphic, or even a large area of white space can be a focal point.

The center of a page (actually, the area just slightly above it) is the most effective location for a focal point because it is the spot people tend to focus on anyway—at least in the Western hemisphere. If the pages are primarily for, say, an Asian audience, an upper right location would be a better focal point because that's the normal center of attention in that part of the world. In this and in other ways, it's important to take your expected users' culture into consideration in Web site design.

In Figure 5-3, the large, bold sans serif header "Building a home?" is the focal point. It grabs the user's attention because of its size and density. The user will naturally go from there to the second-level header ("Let our experience transform your ideas into reality.") because it is in the same typeface and only a slightly smaller size than the first. Finally, the bulleted list in the lower part of the figure draws the reader's attention all the way down the page.

Some general guidelines for achieving contrast with type are:

- Make the differences stark and immediately noticeable.
- Use boldface sparingly because it reduces readability by decreasing the white space between letters.
- Use an underline only when no other alternative will do. It interferes with word shapes and reduces comprehension. Underlines may also be confused as an indication of hyperlink text.
- Contrast a specific point imbedded in other text (for instance, in Figure 5-3, the word "Timberglen" stands out from the surrounding text because it is bold and italic).
- Use a serif typeface for the body of text and sans serif for headers.

Contrast can also be achieved with the use of color. Color may be used to differentiate a heading from its details, to highlight different categories of information, to provide a border around important information, or as a background to establish a tone. The most important use of color in Web design, however, is to emphasize repetition.

Repetition refers to the repeated, consistent use of design elements. When a particular typeface, type size, and type style are applied consistently to a particular level of heading throughout a presentation, the reader will recognize that heading every time it appears. Users assimilate information more easily when repetitive design elements are used. Consistent use of repetition contributes positively to the affect of page design by increasing the ease with which a user becomes familiar and therefore comfortable with a site.

Repeated, consistent use of color is essential to page design. It is consistent use of color, more than contrast or alignment, that ties sets of objects together into threads. Color choices must be applied consistently to Web page backgrounds, text, and hyperlinks. Color choice is also important in distinguishing multimedia options. Repeating a color cues users to similarity of information and design. When color changes, the user is cued in on a change. Consistent use of a color scheme throughout a group of related pages is a good way to tie them together subliminally; users sense the connection without needing to be told in words.

Consistent use of color is also important in establishing a tone appropriate to user expectations. Bold colors—reds, oranges, hot pinks, and purples—heighten emotional tension. These "hot" colors set a tone of intensity, and when used in background color set a tone of anticipation. The more entertaining and emotional your message, the bolder your color choices should be. Muted colors—burgundy, forest green, tans, darker blues—establish feelings of calmness and stability. The more business oriented and serious your message, the more muted your color choices should be.

CHAPTER 5

GO to...

Ambientsoft's site
on the CD-ROM and see how the simple bars provide a focal point and how color is used to contrast headers from text.

GO to...

http://www.tlc.org
to see the fresh, innovative use of color to tie threaded pages on a single topic together.

It's important to be aware of subliminal messages associated with certain colors. The more universal the audience, the more selection should be driven by any meaning often attached to a given color. For instance, red is a "stop" signal in most of the world; using it as a "go" signal for available hyperlinks would violate the user's intuition.

Care in selecting colors is especially important for international audiences. Most North Americans work with 486-generation personal computers (or later) that display 256 colors. The more international your audience, the more likely an eight-color, 386-generation PC will be used. This means that the colors used should be among the primary eight colors; graphics chip differences will distort other colors. This makes the pages a challenge to design but ensures universal consistency in color presentation. (Web browsers always have a default set of colors, but these can be overridden by the page author.)

There are methods of color selection that guarantee consistency across machines of the 486-generation PCs, which support 256 colors. Of the 256 colors available to 486-generation machines, 40 colors vary wildly according to the monitor and the videochip used in the computer. A lovely ochre on one machine might be canary yellow on another and a unattractive brown color on still another. While Netscape and Microsoft Explorer both use a 256-color scheme, because of graphics card variations you cannot predict what users will see unless you use the 216 consistent colors. If you use the 40 variable colors, you cannot anticipate what your user audience will see, and hence, cannot control the affect of the pages. You can avoid color mix-ups by not using the 40 offending color combinations. Photos and other items that use nonsolid colors may also be affected, but there is little you can do to prevent this problem without significant distortion of the photo. In all cases, just to be safe, once colors are decided, you should test your choices on different monitors to see how the pages display.

Note that use of these four principles of text arrangement can result in conflicts. To achieve a high level of contrast, for example, you may sacrifice some level of repetition. Therefore, you need to determine which principle—proximity, alignment, contrast, or repetition—motivates the best arrangement for achieving the overall goals of the presentation.

GO to...

http://www.lynda.com/hexv.html
and
http://www.lynda.com/hexh.html,
which present the consistently viewed and variable-by-monitor colors.

The sites for JCPenney and Neiman Marcus demonstrate how these principles of text arrangement can be used successfully but in different ways to convey a message to the user. The JCPenney site, shown in Figure C-2 (see color insert), uses a centered-text menu bar down the left side, left-justified columns, and subdued, pastel graphics to present a look and feel that is traditional and low-key. The overall impression it gives is stylish (through use of colors), but conservatively so (centered menu and left-justified columns). In contrast, Neiman Marcus's site, as shown in Figure C-3 (see color insert), combines centered text that is left-aligned in a vertical arrangement. It also uses bold, contrasting typefaces and colors. The impression given is that of an active, liberal, fashion leader representative of younger, unmarried, and possibly wealthier users.

Text Grouping

High-volume information requires special consideration. Grouping of information objects with high cardinality is another major composition decision. Suppose the city of New Orleans had a Web page devoted to dining in the city. There are hundreds of restaurants that might be listed, and they might be grouped by name, by type of cuisine, by location in the city, etc. Text composition of information objects of high cardinality requires choosing a grouping, or categorization, format and presenting the information in terms of that format. Several useful categorization formats are location, alphabetic, time, quantitative measure, and presenter-defined.[2]

Location places information objects in a space that may be geographic (as in the location of the French Quarter in a map of the city of New Orleans), symbolic (location of the mayor's office in an organization chart of the city government), physical (location of emergency exits in a manufacturing plant), or systemic (e.g., location of a nerve cell in the human nervous system). Categorization by location answers the question, where?

Alphabetic categorization orders objects by their names—names of products, locations, businesses, people, to name a few. One way to list restaurants on the New Orleans Web site, for instance, would be alphabetically by name. Alphabetic categorization answers the questions, who or what?

Time categorization organizes objects according to their dates or a sequence of chronological events. Time lines are a good way to display historical events, steps in a process, or schedules of activities. Categorizing objects by time answers the question, when?

Quantity categorization positions objects by some numeric amount. For example, prices, distances, revenues, weather, or cubic feet might all be the criteria for ordering a set of objects. Quantitative categorization answers the questions, how much or how many?

The **presenter-defined** categorization groups information objects by some other common attribute or characteristic that the presenter believes users will find valuable. By creating these categories, designers and stewards infuse their own values into the categorization format. In contrast, the other categorization formats are relatively value-free because the classifications are common to most cultures and organizations. For example, restaurants in New Orleans might be categorized by any number of different characteristics—location, alphabetically by name, date established, or average price per entrée. But at times the presenter must make a value judgment on which attribute is most important to the greatest number of users. A reasonable choice in this case might be to categorize by type of food served.

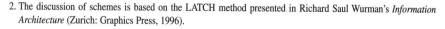

2. The discussion of schemes is based on the LATCH method presented in Richard Saul Wurman's *Information Architecture* (Zurich: Graphics Press, 1996).

So, the essential factor in selecting a method of categorization is the mindset and needs of the intended users. If the designer assumes that restaurant location or name is important to users, then the information should be organized that way. If, on the other hand, users are likely to be interested in type of food, location, or another common characteristic, then a presenter-defined format would be better. The rule is: *Let the users' needs dictate the category.*

One drawback to using a presenter-defined categorization is that, unlike organizing by location, time, alphabet, or quantity, presenter-defined categories rely on some other user understanding of the meaning and use of the format. When a common or popular base of general knowledge does not exist—such as knowledge of food type—the development of a new presenter-defined format may be difficult. New presenter-defined formats require testing with intended users to make sure that the formats will be understood and used successfully. Once such a format is decided, it provides the basis of Web page design for that particular information.

GO to...   **http://superpages.gte.com**
to see an innovative site on restaurants developed for GTE Interactive in conjunction with Yahoo. While not addressing all of the possible categories mentioned, it allows the user to search for many combinations of geography, food type, and price selection. Each restaurant retrieved can then have its menu (exact food offered and prices) retrieved for review. Finally, once a destination is selected, the user can request a map and select either the most direct or the fastest route to the restaurant. Maps can be generated from any point in the United States to any other point in the United States. This site makes very effective and affective use of the information available to it.

Storyboarding

The text composition process often draws on a technique known as storyboarding, which is frequently used in advertising and filmmaking. A **storyboard** is a display of a series of pictures with text on a "board" (piece of cardboard or paper) that tells a "story." In a storyboard for a Web presentation, the pictures and text represent each information object as well as all of the information pertaining to linkages, cardinality, and volatility. Once fully developed, a storyboard also contains references for graphics, tables, maps, photos, and other multimedia. (These later additions are discussed in Chapters 6 and 7.) Storyboards map out what users will see and do on every Web page. Storyboarding is a useful way to organize Web information into pages and to understand the user threads that weave them together.

Once the complete set of Web pages has been represented in a group of storyboards, the pages are arranged in the order in which users are expected to view them. One way to develop a storyboard is to create the text Web presentation completely on 3x5 cards, as can be done for the information structure diagram. Then the entire presentation can be arranged to show the main relationships. For very large presentations, storyboards for each presentation thread can be analyzed individually, then together. There is software available to automate this process, such as Storywalls by Cost Technology.

After all the storyboard pages have been laid out, they should be analyzed one by one as each thread is followed through the information. You may notice gaps to be filled by additional information or the need to rearrange some information objects. If using index cards, move the cards around, experimenting with different threads to present the clearest paths through the material. You will find that, even with the information structure diagram and prose for all objects, there is a surprising amount of choice remaining on specific words to be placed on each page and on the way to weave information objects together.

Storyboards let you experiment with alternative wordings and arrangements at little cost. Once a coherent, understandable story can be traced down each thread, the next step is testing. Taking the point of view of each expected user group, walk through the material. If the message is not consistent and effective for each thread, revise the information and retest other overlapping threads, as needed.

Note that some information is viewed by all users, while other information might be viewed by only a few. Web pages for information objects with few users can be tailored to meet the particular mental model and needs of the select group of users who access them. The Web pages that all viewers will see must be designed for broad appeal. The home page, for instance, is seen by all viewers and is usually a table of contents for more detailed information at lower levels.

Page Formatting

Page formatting refers to methods of screen presentation and the division of space on a page. The alternatives include menus, maps, and frames.

Menus provide a list of information objects for selection by a user in the form of a single column, a single column with indented subentries, multiple columns, or tables. Initial home page designs often take the form of a menu that provides access to the rest of a site through text entries.

Figure 5-4 shows the menu for the Mars Introduction page, which is in the form of a single column with indented subentries. A large-print header identifying the page is followed by simple text with hyperlinks to other locations in the site. Although the page is wordy and uninteresting, it does meet the criteria of providing enough information for the surfer to determine whether or not to continue to view the presentation.

A variation on this mostly text type of home page is the multicolumn table. This results in a smaller-sized page, with another level of menu page required to present all information.

Menus are easy to design, simple to maintain, and fast to load to a user computer. Creating menus requires no additional technical skills—hardware or software—beyond those required by basic HTML. Menus work best with text objects consisting of one line of text, preferably under five words each. They are often used in sites that contain extensive lists of hyperlinks on their home page. Menus are used to format such pages in the interest of keeping navigational efficiency high by having only a few levels of detail.

Mars Introduction

Where there is no vision, the people perish.
- Proverbs 29:18

Table of Contents

- **Mars Introduction Page (This Page)**
  - ☐ Introduction
  - ☐ Mars Statistics
  - ☐ Animations of Mars
  - ☐ Views of Mars
  - ☐ Mars Moon Summary
- **Pathfinder Images**
- **Selected Images from Mars Pathfinder**
- **Life from Mars: The Discovery**
  - ☐ Statement from Daniel S. Goldin
  - ☐ Meteorite Yields Evidence of Primitive Life on Early Mars
  - ☐ Life from Mars: Video Animations
- **Martian Volcanoes**
- **Martian Clouds**
- **The Surface of Mars**
- **The Face on Mars**
- **Satellites of Mars**
  - ☐ Deimos and Phobos
- **The Rationale for Exploring Mars**
- **Chronology of Mars Exploration**
- **Project Viking Fact Sheet**

Figure 5-4   Menu page format

http://www.sony.com
where Sony Corp. presents an artfully designed text home page. The main menu items are listed in text and can be seen by anyone using a standard Web browser, thus meeting the criteria of having all key information immediately visible. This text screen, while not exciting, is an elegant combination of menu, color, and graphics.

Convenient as they are, menus tend to be boring. They have very low affectiveness, even though effectiveness and navigational efficiency can both be high. However, as the Sony page shows, menus can be elegant when designed with the appropriate combination of color and graphics. Menu formats are always used for text-only Web pages designed for low-tech users. In fact, out of consideration to users with no graphics capability, every site should have one set of pages designed in a text-only, menu format as an alternative to tables, maps, or frames.

Another page format option is an image map, or map. A **map** overlays a graphic with text and contains graphical hyperlink areas, called **hot regions**, that you click to access other Web locations. Figure 5-5 shows the map used in a privately owned site intended to promote Dallas as a diverse city that is pro-business and a great place to live.

Figure 5-5 Map page format

Maps are quite affective and can present a unique view of the page topic in a way that words cannot express. The main advantage of maps is non-scrolled viewing to the site's hyperlinks. The disadvantage of maps is that they can get quite complex and large. The larger and more complex, the longer the map will take to load to the viewer's computer. During particularly busy times of day, the loading time can seem like eternity and will turn off many viewers. Keep in mind that, in addition to the map format for the Web page, a text version of the page will need to be provided for low-tech users, and this doubling of design-time cost may be considered too much.

The third variation of page format is to divide the display area into separately controlled sub-areas called frames. **Frames** divide a Web page into windows that function independently of one another, much like the "picture in a picture" sometimes seen on TV. A Web page might define three frames, containing a menu in one, a header in another, and details in the other (see Figure 5-6). Frames are used when some information must remain on the screen while other Web pages are being viewed. They allow for the simultaneous display of information from several different Web objects.

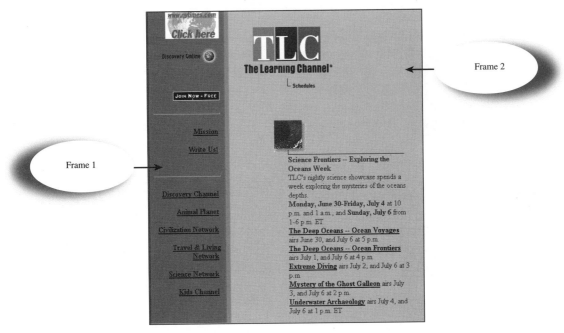

Figure 5-6 Framed page format

GO to...

http://www.pointcast.com and download its free personal information presentation software.

While there is no technical limit to the number of frames on a screen, some very complex sites, like PointCast broadcasts, can be confusing because of the volume of information in multiple frames that are all changing.

Frames can accommodate all multimedia types as well as menus and maps. They require no additional software or hardware and are viewable by all browsers supporting the HTML 3.0 standard.[3] With careful design, frames can improve on text or text with graphics menus. For instance, the menu arrows in the top frame of the first screen in Figure C-4 (see color insert) change both color and direction to show user location. On this screen—the home page for Exercise, Inc.—more information about the company is indicated by a down arrow (next to the far left menu choice, "Exercise, Inc."). On the second screen, the arrows at the top change direction and the arrows on the secondary side menu change color and direction to show location. This capability greatly reduces navigational problems associated with losing a thread as the user moves from one page to another.

3. HTML and other Web standards are developed by a group called the World Wide Web Consortium, or W3C. The W3C is a global, voluntary group funded by industry and government. The new HTML standard (4.0) and more information on W3C can be found at http://www.w3c.org/

Deciding on the number of frames to include and their locations requires careful planning. The main problem related to frame design is that the "main message" of the site, usually found in the atomic information object pages, has a smaller viewing area since it will be within a frame within the display area. Usually, menu choices remain on the screen while other information in other frames changes. (See Figure C-4.) Because the amount of information that can be presented in a single Web frame is limited, more screens may be needed and more complex navigation may therefore be required of the user if he or she is to scroll to all desired information. Here trade-offs are made between the need for screen and frame size to provide effective and affective design, and the need for increased navigational simplicity. In Figure C-4, all the material presented in the "main" frame fits horizontally in the frame. Only vertical scrolling is required. If the information required both horizontal and vertical scrolling, trade-offs would have to be made. Finally, because frames are not available to users lacking the support of HTML 3.0-capable browsers, it's a good idea to maintain a text version of the Web site.

There is no one right answer to the question of when to use menus, maps, or frames in page format. They may be used singly or together to good effect. Typically, first-generation Web page formats use menus, and second-generation menus include graphics and possibly tables. Succeeding generations of the presentation tend to move toward either maps or frames as designers become more proficient with the information. Experimentation is important in determining which page format fits your intended user audience best.

Page Evaluation

After the text pages have been composed, each should be reviewed with the stewards and presenters to determine their accuracy and effectiveness. Evaluations can be formal or informal. Each page and its links should be treated as a straw man, or opponent, to be defeated. The group should be as critical as possible about the page contents and design—in a good-humored way, of course. The purpose of evaluation is to judge how well the Web pages have achieved overall goals and objectives in light of the general presentation criteria for effectiveness, affectiveness, and navigational efficiency. Evaluation provides feedback through which it is possible to change the original conceptions of the Web project if they have been improperly stated. Evaluation also provides "feedforward" to generate new goals and requirements as the Web presentation takes shape.

The evaluation activity can be conducted in many ways. Typically, the group reviews the results of the activities one at a time, looking for flaws, gaps, misstatements, poor aesthetics, and the like and correcting them. The designer records changes and recommendations and uses them to adjust the design. One of the reasons this activity is essential is that stewards and presenters frequently change their mind after they see the first working model, or prototype, of the Web pages. Earlier decisions about information object grouping, formatting, and design may change in light of seeing the pages on a display screen.

Essentially, a **prototype** is an incomplete but working onscreen version of the Web pages. It's a good idea to develop a prototype to test and revise the design as it takes shape. Prototypes are used to provide the visual and interactive experiences that are not easily defined in words. Early in a project, a storyboard might be sketched out on paper or a collection of index cards. As the Web presentation design nears completion, a prototype is developed to implement the storyboards as a means of obtaining design feedback. Prototypes are useful for:

- evaluating threads and ensuring closure
- evaluating the usefulness of multimedia and their integration into the Web page
- proving that a design concept works

Prototypes are more useful in uncovering fundamental flaws in these areas than a paper storyboard. If serious changes are suggested as a result of the evaluation, additional prototypes might be developed and evaluated.

Prototypes rarely contain the entire contents of a Web presentation. For instance, if a company's Web site is to present product information, a prototype can be created that represents the Web pages showing specifications for two of the 50 products to be in the final presentation. This prototype is then tested and, if improvements are warranted, revised. Once a sound standard for presenting product specifications is established for this particular presentation, the Web pages detailing the specifications for the full product line can be developed. The prototype continues to be modified as more information about the project is obtained and additional user reactions to the design are needed.

Every generation of the Web presentation should also be tested by potential users, either individually or in focus groups. The outside perspective almost always uncovers misinterpretations or faulty design assumptions made by insiders. For example, an arrangement of text that looked natural to the stewards and designer because it was based on the layout used in internal documents may, in fact, be off-putting or unnatural to external users, who have not seen those documents. Although in a sense evaluation never really ends, the evaluation activity may be considered complete when no more obvious or necessary improvements can be made.

The Text Composition Process: A Walkthrough

Now you are familiar with text design components and techniques. In this section we review the complete process to show how the components and techniques fit together in practice.

The first step in the text composition process is to decide on overall page format—whether to use a single menu display, maps, frames, or a combination of them. The information objects to be placed on each page are selected according to the hierarchy of information objects and the storyboard(s) created in earlier steps. Then, information is arranged, beginning with the definition of the focal point, which is usually a heading.

Text for headings and hyperlinks are developed as page elements for the final arrangement are decided. The time put into this text creation is well spent because it largely determines continuation of viewing. Usually, as text has been developed for each information object, a few key words are identified and annotated on 3x5 cards or in an outline. These key words provide the basis for developing text for headings and hyperlinks.

After the focal point is designed and heading and hyperlink text created, the remainder of the presentation is designed to provide visually stimulating pages that convey the desired affective message. The arrangement of pages and the objects on the pages follows the overall composition guidelines on proximity, alignment, contrast, and repetition.

An overall design for header placement and style, for more detailed text, for type of bullets, and so on should be created for all pages. Each level of header should use repetitive elements (to establish continuity with itself) and contrasting elements (sufficient to distinguish itself from other levels). Other important information should be differentiated in type style (bold or italic), color, or face. For example, a 36-point header of Arial Black typeface could be used to introduce all major topics. The topics could be differentiated from each other by using different background colors and text colors. Bulleted lists and lists with indentations are familiar techniques for summarizing key points, especially for business information.

One issue that arises during the composition process concerns Web page length. (Keep in mind that when frames are the format choice, this discussion applies equally to the collection of frames seen as a unit on screen as well as to each individual frame.) Ideally, each page should be fully visible in a single 640 x 480 screen size display, approximately 6 x 4 inches, as mentioned earlier in the chapter. Anything larger will require scrolling, which can be annoying to the user. One rule of thumb is to apply the principle of proximity in keeping related objects together. If scrolling is then needed, so be it; composition will proceed easily and logically from one object to the next. If the proximity between the items is loose, however, or the items can be decomposed and arranged a different way, then multiple page designs should be considered.

Recall that the general guideline is to keep text short, informative, and complete enough for the viewers to determine if they want to continue navigating the site. The shortest home page would include only introductory information about the presenting organization; however, such a design would not meet the completeness criteria. Therefore, the shortest home page that is also informative and complete enough includes introductory information plus enough other information for the user to decide where on the site to go next.

During development of the information structure diagram, each object was assigned its cardinality. The number of object occurrences is used in deciding the criterion for keeping information "short." While there are no absolutes, one rule of thumb is that no page should be longer than two or three screens of information. This implies a practical limit of about 120 lines of information plus separator lines. Thus, if the cardinality of an object were 25 or more, and each object was several lines of text, some information might best be relocated at a lower level or perhaps summarized in a different way. Information objects with cardinalities over 10 frequently require grouping and the use of within-page links, or even separation of the information on multiple pages. (Notice that many FAQ, or frequently asked questions, pages violate this guideline.)

5

CHAPTER

As mentioned above, the time sensitivity of information might also be an issue. In general, highly volatile information should be loaded directly to the Web from a separately maintained database. Such information should be located on pages at a lower level of detail and occur only once within a group of related pages so that information changed affects only a single Web page. (Keep your Web site goals in mind in making this decision, however, because this rule is often broken. Pages that feature news, as discussed earlier, place the most volatile information on the first page in a prominent position for continuous updating.)

Several other items of information should be incorporated into the presentation at the end of this phase of Web design. They are the disclaimer, date of last update, and contact information, and they should be placed on the bottom of every Web page developed, whether personal or for an organization.

Disclaimers are usually provided to protect the presenter from invasion by pranksters who fool around with the contents or to make clear the information presented is not legally binding, that is, the presenter is not guaranteeing the accuracy of the information presented, such as financial information. The date of last update is important to allow the user to decide whether the currency of information warrants further review. Finally, contact information provides page closure, allowing the user to contact the organization with no need for additional work (or page viewing). Contact information generally includes an e-mail address for immediate communication with the presenting organization.

When all composition for the Web presentation is complete, it is evaluated once more. During this evaluation, the stewards and designers present the complete design for walkthrough by audiences that might include peers and prospective users.

The above work represents a first-generation Web design completed by most developers when they are about to move from paper-based to Web-based pages. A first-generation design is the basis for multimedia decisions to augment the text, and it becomes the version of the page used by the nongraphical browsers that serve most of the world.

 W e b   D e s i g n   i n   t h e   R e a l   W o r l d

Best Personalized Books

Before developing a prototype of the Best Web site, Sue and Wendy met to develop page headers, hyperlink text, a short description of the company for the home page, and introductions to each major information object topic. To do this they analyzed each information object from the structure diagram to identify the main ideas to be presented on each page. Jack, acting as a presenter, periodically reviewed and commented on what they developed.

Rather than include the entire dialog during which Sue and Wendy reviewed the presentation, which took about six hours, only the discussion of the alternatives for the home page are included here.

Wendy and Sue spent several hours working on the text for the home page. Text for other pages was to be selected from existing brochures, with the understanding that wording would be reevaluated in the prototype (which Sue had decided to put together on screen), since people react differently to text on a screen than on a page.

Initially, Wendy had envisioned the home page as having a photo or graphic with a heading identifying the company and links to the next set of pages. Sue explained that some key words, or main ideas, expressing what Best was and why anyone would want to become a user were needed to draw surfers into the site. She reminded Wendy that the first seven seconds determine whether or not a surfer becomes a user. It's all they need to develop their emotional reaction to the company. Therefore, the home page is crucial in drawing the intended audience to the site. Jack and Wendy agreed.

A set of ideas to be presented on the home page were defined initially as:

- start your own business

- work from home

- be your own boss

The introductory sentence Sue and Wendy developed combined these ideas: "Start a business at home—Be your own boss."

As Sue and Wendy talked further, they decided that this sentence did not say anything about the "work" of being a licensee and could relate to virtually any franchising or licensing business. They then developed a second list of important ideas, selected

from the source material gathered earlier. The second list is shown in Figure 5-8 and has several main ideas with sub-ideas. These were not all used on the home page, but they were kept for possible use on later pages. Notice that these vital ideas summarize key points *about* information objects but are *not* themselves information objects. Rather, they are descriptive information about Best Personalized Books, which, in this instance, is itself the information object. That is, the information object on which the home page is based is the entire company to a surfer.

```
Start a business at home
    Business opportunity
    Be your own boss
High profit margin
Low start-up cost
Market the product
    On location
    From home
Products
    Foreign languages
    Customized books
    Licensed special characters (e.g., Disney)
    Product demand
Licensing
    No markets saturated
    Cost
    How to get started
    Minimum computer configuration
Best Personalized Books
    Trustworthy
    Established (e.g., not likely to go out of business)
```

Figure 5-7
Ideas for Best's home page

The list of ideas in Figure 5-7 demonstrates the flexibility site designers have in final content and design of a Web page. These summary points about Best cannot all fit on a single screen and have high affect. The designers and stewards needed to decide what essential ideas serve to describe the company and its products, all the while appealing to the licensees and surfers who might buy books or become licensees.

In talking about how best to describe the company and the business opportunity, Sue and Wendy further developed assumptions about both current and potential licensees. First, they assumed that both groups would also look at competitors' Web sites. Second, the appeal of the site had to be global. This meant attention to wording and color choices as well as multi-lingual presentation. The first generation of pages would be in English, but subsequent generations would include French, Spanish, and some kanji-type (e.g., Japanese) language. Third, some indication of the scope of products and the simplicity of the book personalizing process was required. For the first-generation site especially, the writing had to be very simple for people with limited ability to read English. *Therefore, the goals of the introductory sentence and page were to distinguish Best from its competition while providing a specific definition of the type of licensing involved, appealing to the global audience, and giving enough information to encourage further viewing.*

Having established this goal for the home page, Sue and Wendy developed more alternatives for the introductory sentence from the list in Figure 5-8. They kept returning to this statement of purpose throughout the entire composition process. Then they generated a list of possible sentences to express this key home page goal. These sentences are listed in Figure 5-8.

```
Create your own company.
Create your own company with your computer.
Create your own company with your computer developing
 personalized books.
Make personalized books at home.
Develop personalized books with your computer.
Make money with your computer.
With your computer and laser printer, you can personalize books
 at home.
Personalize books with your computer.
Personalize books at home.
Personalize books at home with your computer.
Personalize children's books with a computer.
Develop children's books in your spare time.
Develop personalized children's books in your spare time.
Develop personalized children's books in your spare time with
 your computer.
Personalize children's books with a computer in your spare time.
Personalize children's books with a computer from your home.
```

Figure 5-8
Introductory sentence alternatives

Initially, they selected the last sentence shown in Figure 5-8: "Personalize children's books with a computer from your home." By the time a storyboard of the page was created, though, the text was changed to "Personalize children's books with a computer in your spare time." It took about 1½ hours to obtain the nine essential words. The team still didn't love it, but decided it was acceptable for the time being.

This introductory sentence was to be followed by a few others: "For more information about this exciting opportunity, click one of the buttons below. To see the easy process, click here. Best products are currently in 15 languages and 41 countries—7 book product lines and growing." In contrast to the first sentence, these sentences took about ten minutes to write.

The rest of the meeting was devoted to developing specific wording for the hypertext that would be clicked to reach other pages on the site. After about 15 minutes of discussion, the team decided that the most simple, direct terms were best. The options are shown in Figure 5-9.

All of the above constituted the main part of the text analysis stage. After the message content had been temporarily finalized, the team progressed quickly through the text composition stage. The text version of the home page, the first to be seen by a visitor to the site, is shown in Figure C-5 (see color insert). There was little disagreement about the ordering of the items in the list. There was also no disagreement that this page was not what the Kalishers really had in mind. The information presented in Figure C-5 became the basis for the next, graphically oriented version of the same page (discussed in Chapter 7).

The Best Personalized Books text home page meets the criteria for being short, informative, and complete. On a printed page, the information looks acceptable for business and incorporates the design elements of proximity, alignment, contrast, and repetition. One problem with the page is obvious: on a computer screen, it would not be visually compelling. It has the requisite information, but it is boring. The home page rates high in effect and low in affect. The later inclusion of graphics and multimedia would improve page affect (discussed in Chapter 7). But hyperlink analysis and composition needed to come next (Chapter 6). Notice that the disclaimer at the bottom of the home page provides a means of immediate access via e-mail and gives the organization's address, phone, and date of last update. In addition, a request for reporting of incorrect or offensive information is provided.

User	Option	Wording
Book Buyer	Purchase a single book	Buy a book?
Potential Licensee	How to become a licensee	Become a dealer?
Potential/Current Licensees	Marketing	How to sell Best products
Potential/Current Licensees	Learning about the company	Who is Best?
Potential/Current Licensees	Current events	What's new at Best?
Current Licensees	Support & sales	Current licensee area

Figure 5-9
Hyperlink wording options

S u m m a r y

In the text analysis phase, every information object is examined independently and prose is written to describe its main idea and supporting ideas, if any. The criteria here are for completeness and accuracy above all else. The text is reviewed by several audiences and rewritten to address problems. The outcome of this step is complete text descriptions of each information object.

Text composition is accomplished by means of five activities: arrangement, grouping, storyboarding, page format, and evaluation. During arrangement, typography, layout, and color are decided based on the principles of proximity, alignment, contrast, and repetition. According to the principles of proximity, information objects that relate should be placed together. Fairly volatile objects are often composed according to this principle.

The alignment principle guides the use of left, right, and centered justification of objects on a page. Contrast is the use of different design elements, such as typeface, type size, or color to identify a focal point or to identify different levels of information. Repetition defines consistency of format through the use of repeated design elements. Typeface, type size, text alignment, and color can all be used to establish repetition.

During grouping, categories of information are defined to give the user easier access to it. The formats for categorization include location, alphabet, time, quantitative measures, and presenter-defined.

Storyboarding is the development of a series of sketches showing the text composition of each page. A story should be developed for each thread of defined use to ensure that all necessary links are developed.

Page format can be determined using menus, maps, and frames or a combination of them. There are pros and cons to using each method. In any case, a low-tech, text-only version of Web pages should be developed for people around the world who cannot access Web pages using frames, maps, or other advanced design elements.

Overall, the text composition phase proceeds for all information objects contained within the information object diagram. When text composition is complete, it is evaluated for its efficacy in meeting the overall goals of the Web presentation and the goals for each user group.

R e v i e w   Q u e s t i o n s

1. A company has used the same brochure successfully for four years. Can it be placed on the Web "as is"? Why or why not?

2. What problems are created for presenters if any of the seven writing goals (for example, completeness or accuracy) is not met?

3. What general purpose is served by selection of certain typefaces and type styles for a Web site?

4. From a user's point of view, why is the principle of proximity helpful? What about alignment? contrast? repetition?

5. Describe four different ways that information about two schools (e.g., a high school and a college) might be categorized. Who would the expected users of these sites be? How do different user needs or interests influence your choice of categories?

6. Debate the topic: It is better to have too much text on a page rather than too little.

7. Name five ways in which repetition can be used in text composition.

8. What is storyboarding? How is it used in developing Web sites?

9. What is a focal point, and why is it important? How does focal point relate to page layout and information grouping?

10. What are the advantages and disadvantages of maps, frames, and menus in determining Web page format?

P r o j e c t s

1. Visit L. L. Bean (http://www.llbean.com) and Lands' End (http://www.landsend.com) Web sites. Compare and contrast their respective home pages, pages on flannel shirts, and ordering pages in terms of information grouping and the use of page layout design principles.

2. Surf the Web and find examples of pages that show good and poor use of typography, layout, proximity, alignment, contrast, repetition, and color. Can you find a site that violates all of the guidelines? What is its affect? Effect? Navigational efficiency?

3. Review the "after" design in Figure 5-3 and identify the design principles you think were used to create it. List them, and then explain why or why not you would have used each one. What would you have done with the text instead?

C a s e   P r o j e c t

1. For each information object identified in the information structure diagram for your project, identify its main idea and write clear concise text to express it. Keep track of the time spent in this exercise and the number of wording alternatives you develop for key sentences. Do this with the appropriate information steward(s), if possible.

2. Create a storyboard for each Web page in your presentation, indicating where on each page each item of text will be placed. Specify the typeface, size, and style for each item. Indicate for each page how the principles of proximity, alignment, contrast, and repetition are used.

3. Review your work using the storyboard technique of walking through each story line with the information stewards and organization presenter. If possible, also select two viewers of differing interests and walk them through your storyboards.

4. Define your overall strategy for the composition of the home page and each succeeding level of pages. Show that your threads can be maintained visually and emotionally through your use of typography, frames, maps, text, and the design guidelines of proximity, alignment, repetition, and contrast. Obtain reviewer comments and improve your pages accordingly. Then, create the text version of your pages.

F u r t h e r   R e a d i n g

- Bain, Steve, and Daniel Gray. *Looking Good Online.* Indianapolis, Ind.: Ventana Press, 1997.

- Barzun, Jacques. *Simple & Direct.* New York: Harper and Row, 1980.

- Ladd, Eric, and Jim O'Donnell. *Using HTML 3.2, Java 1.1, and CGI*, platinum ed. Indianapolis, Ind.: Que Corporation, 1996.

- Parker, Roger C. *One Minute Designer.* Indianapolis, Ind.: Que Corporation, 1993.

- _____, with Carrie Beverly. *Looking Good in Print.* Research Triangle Park, N.C.: Ventana Press, 1997.

- Rabb, Margaret Y. *The Presentation Design Book,* 1st and 2d eds. Chapel Hill, N.C.: Ventana Press, 1990, 1993.

- Sano, Darrell. *Designing Large-Scale Web Sites: A Visual Design Methodology.* New York: John Wiley & Sons, 1997.

- Strunk, W., Jr., and E. B. White. *The Elements of Style.* New York: Macmillan, 1952.

- Williams, Robin. *The Non-designer's Design Book.* Berkeley, Calif.: Peachpit Press, 1994.

- Zinsser, William. *On Writing Well.* New York: Harper and Row, 1980.

6

Linkage Analysis and Composition

In This Chapter You Will Learn To:

- Describe the three types of hyperlinks: intrapage, intrasite, and intersite
- Explain the role hyperlinks play in organizing and presenting information
- Determine the appropriate number of hyperlinks to incorporate into a site
- Evaluate hyperlinks for changes they may bring about in information chunking
- Finalize the phrasing to be used for hyperlinks
- Explain the logic for applying color to hyperlinks

W e b   D e s i g n   i n   t h e   R e a l   W o r l d

Best Personalized Books

Earlier analysis established the need for a variety of user threads, for current and potential licensees and for single book buyers. Given the differing information requirements of each potential user group, it was clear that the site would have to contain multiple pages of different kinds. Jack was concerned that both prospective and existing franchisees be able to move quickly through the site to get to the information they wanted. This meant that the site would be woven together by means of a network of hyperlinks.

Both Jack and Wendy wanted the hyperlinks to be simple, intuitive, and visually appealing. Sue led a review of each business function to be presented to ensure that the team had identified all of the threads needed. Each jumping-off point (the initial hyperlink in the thread) was marked on printed copies of the current version of the prototype. Also, the phrasing for hyperlinks developed during text composition was reevaluated to ensure that users would understand what information could be found at the destination.

Overview: Linkage Analysis and Composition

In Chapter 5 you learned how to analyze and compose text pages. The text pages by themselves, however, are not a Web site. They become a Web site only after the establishment of hyperlinks. During **linkage analysis**, hyperlinks are defined for information objects within the site and are "threaded" to each other, and sometimes to other Web sites. The links are then reevaluated to make sure they have not affected information content or the way it is likely to be interpreted. During **linkage composition**, precise phrasing is chosen for each link, and the links are actually incorporated into the Web presentation. Linkage text color is then selected and applied.

Key Roles

Both information stewards and designers participate in linkage analysis and selection, but designers perform the programming required to implement hyperlinks. Both designers and information stewards evaluate the links for navigational efficiency. Stewards have final approval of link selection and phrasing because they have the most knowledge of the presentation contents. They are best qualified to assess what value links may add (or not add) to that content. Stewards also have final approval because they are the ones who are ultimately responsible for the Web presentation.

Linkage Analysis Guidelines

Recall that a **hyperlink**, or **link**, establishes an electronic connection between two Web information objects, creating the threads that tie information objects together. Hyperlinks afford movement between two points: from a jumping-off point to a destination point. They are a powerful and distinctive capability of the Web, weaving many different areas of information together and making it possible to navigate through page content in ways that are impossible in other media.

There are three kinds of hyperlinks:

1. **Intrapage hyperlinks** move the user from one position on a page to another position on the same page, keeping the user at exactly the same URL, or address. Recall from Chapter 1 that a URL is the name for a Web page. Each Web page has its own URL, consisting of a computer identification called the Web domain name, one or more directories, and an information object identifier. (Refer to Figure 1-1 to review the components of a URL.) The text information that a user clicks onscreen refers to a URL for an information object. Intrapage hyperlinks reference chunks of text used, for example, to link each item in a list of frequently asked questions (FAQs) to its answer on the same page. (Recall from Chapter 1 the FAQ page in the Planetary Society Web site. See Figure 1-2.)

2. **Intrasite hyperlinks** move the user from an information object on one page to an information object on another page in the same Web site.

3. **Intersite, or free, hyperlinks** transport the user to other organizations' Web presentations located anywhere on the Web.

All three types of hyperlinks are illustrated in Figure 6-1.

Intrapage Hyperlinks

Intrapage hyperlinks are developed to simplify access to information in long, complex Web pages. Any information object evaluated for categorical information grouping is a candidate for intrapage links. Each category—location, alphabet, time, quantitative measure, and presenter-defined—should be assessed. Figure 6-2 shows alphabetically ordered items linked via intrapage hyperlinks. The intrapage hyperlinks connect a letter of the alphabet with a list of restaurants whose name begins with that letter. Once they arrive at the alphabetic category, users can go to restaurant Web sites, if they are available. For instance, clicking a "C" at the top of the Web page jumps the user to the "C" set of listings. Within the "C" group, Chez Henri has a Web site that might be visited.

Whether the links are organized alphabetically or according to another format (say, in the restaurant example, according to the type of food offered—Chinese, fast food, Italian, etc.), the way in which they are presented is essentially the same. In this format, the hyperlinks are listed at the top of the Web page. Each element in the list is a user-defined, on-page hyperlink that will take the user to a corresponding location farther down the page. The user has the option of using the links to jump to a location, or simply scrolling through all of the information to the end of the page.

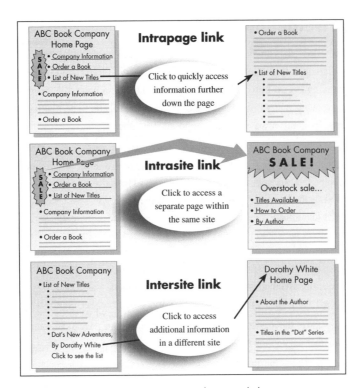

Figure 6-1 Intrapage, intrasite, and intersite links

Intrasite Hyperlinks

Intrasite hyperlinks are used for three purposes. First, they compose the threads that tie presentation pages together in ways that are meaningful to users. Second, they provide the links between business relationships. Third, intrasite hyperlinks provide an alternative to intrapage hyperlinks when the information to be presented is too long for a single Web page (150 lines of text is usually the upper limit for any given Web page).

As shown in Figure 6-1, an intrasite hyperlink might be used to satisfy the needs of a user looking for a bargain book. Clicking the "SALE" hyperlink allows the user to quickly jump from the home page to the overstock SALE page. To continue along the thread, the user could click another intrasite link to view the available book titles or authors, or go directly to an order page. This could be a useful thread for a user who wants to quickly order a book on sale.

An intrasite link can also be used to facilitate relationships between the different business functions within the organization. The ABC Book Company might format part of its home page to include intrasite links to the customer service department, order department, or marketing department and include intrasite links on each of *those* pages to access the other departments.

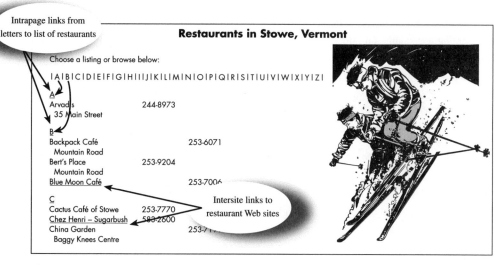

Figure 6-2   Alphabetically-ordered identifiers and hyperlinks

Finally, an intrasite link might be selected to better organize information when there are too many information objects to fit on a single Web page. When this is the case, the information objects are categorized, and each category of information placed on a separate page. These pages are then linked together using intrasite links. In the ABC Book example, the company may have thousands of books available for purchase. They could categorize the books according to type—mystery, romance, etc.—and place each category on its own page. They could even have one separate reference Web page that simply lists the intrasite links. Click to view:

- Mystery
- Romance

Each hyperlink relates to a different URL, which in turn identifies a specific Web page.

When deciding whether to go with an intrapage or intrasite hyperlink, there are several things to consider. Both have their advantages and disadvantages. In general, it is easier to maintain a single Web page than it is to maintain many pages, simply because it is easier to track a single item. Using this argument, a single Web page with intrapage hyperlinks is preferred for lists of items with fewer than 150 lines of text.

Another factor affecting the decision is that amount of load time and volume of information on Web pages are related. The less information on a page, the faster it will be displayed. The more information, the longer the display time. The same arguments apply to printing—short pages print faster than long pages. The question is, *How long is long?* All things being equal, any Web page with more than three screens of information (again, totaling about 150 lines, or 50 or so lines per screen of formatted text), or taking more than 15 seconds to display under ideal conditions, is a candidate for multipage storage.

Expected uses of a page also make a difference. A Web page might be used for simple viewing or for printing. Depending on how much of the information the user would want, single or multiple pages and hyperlinks would be selected. Returning to the book example, a viewer might want to print information on only one or two books, in which case a separate Web page for each book would be preferred. But if a viewer wants to browse all books regardless of classification, a single page would be preferred. This is another example of the importance of knowing the user's wants and needs.

Intersite Hyperlinks

Each Web page, on its own, should provide a complete message that adds to a user need or goal. However, users always want more information than can fit on one Web page, or sometimes even within one Web presentation. This is where intersite, or free, hyperlinks can be useful.

Creativity, expertise of the steward, and goal-oriented Web surfing can be used to identify intersite hyperlinks. The purpose of free hyperlinks is to use the content of other organizations' Web presentations to enhance your own. The creativity requires something called new media thinking. If we think in a traditional, paper-bound way, we ask only for more information of the same kind, perhaps in more detail, from other presentations, the goal being to supplement our own information. **New media thinking** asks us to go beyond the confines of the information we have, to explore new but related topic areas. There is no limit to the sites that can provide such information.

For instance, suppose a surfing expedition for "safari tours" returned a reference to the Urban Safari Wear site (http://www.laig.com/safari/). This site sells clothing that is traditional to safaris—khaki bush jackets, pants, etc. But the company's Web site offers more than information on its clothing. Its developers included several pages of intersite hyperlinks to broaden the site's appeal. The resources to which hyperlinks are provided include U.S. State Department pages for visas and passports; pages on travel warnings from the State Department and the Centers for Disease Control; and weather reports for global locations including Africa. In addition, a list of U.S. travel and tour operators that offer African safaris is provided. Finally, excerpts from several books on culture, customs, animal habits, and other interesting topics are provided on a Web page called "Africa from A to Z." This variety of topics will appeal to a broad audience, some of whom might be more willing to purchase their clothing from this company than from a company that simply sells clothes.

Each member of the Web development team can help search for potential free link sites. Involving many people of different interests and objectives is important in identifying free hyperlinks because more link sites of greater variety will be identified. As sites are identified, each is examined for its ability to enhance the effect and affect of the "home" presentation. Each site selected as a possible link then needs to be evaluated to determine if it meets the following criteria:

- The information on the site is complete.
- The information on the site is accurate.
- The relationship with the site works to your company's or organization's competitive advantage.

- The tone of the site is compatible with that of your company.
- The site appeals to your expected audience.
- The site supports or enhances the goal of a particular page in the presentation or the presentation's overall goal.

Free hyperlinks are useful only if they lead to information that is valuable, interesting, relevant, or helpful to the person visiting the site. Ultimately, intersite hyperlinks should lead to viewer-to-user conversion, thread completion, or sale "closure." Retired American Airlines Chief Information Officer Max Hopper refers to the "look-to-book ratio" of the airlines' automated services. When a traveler merely looks at flight information in American's Web site, it costs the company money. Booking, or selling a seat, is always the goal and closes a thread. The goal of thread closure must be at the forefront of free link selection. The last thing you want to do is casually direct a potential user to another site that might have more appeal than your own.

The major benefit of intersite links is that another organization's pages are providing source information (at no cost to you) that is more accurate and current than you could provide and maintain. However, both a benefit and a risk of intersite links is that you, as the presenter, have no maintenance responsibility for the information at these sites. This is a benefit since there is always a cost involved in maintenance. It is a risk because changes made to the site at any time might alter your message unintentionally; constant checking of the continued relevance of these hyperlinks is required.

Some legal battles—for instance, Ticketron versus Microsoft—are being fought over the use of free links without the permission of the site's owner. For the time being, the consensus is that they are legal.

Rationale for Selecting Hyperlinks

All three types go through similar processes of analysis, evaluation, and composition; what is different for each type of link is the criteria it must meet to be selected. As shown in Figure 6-3, intrapage links are generally selected for their ability to speed users' navigation or to help users access information. Intrasite hyperlinks complete threads or document business relationships, for instance, by bringing the user to the location on the site that provides information on customer support policies and procedures. Intersite hyperlinks are selected based on the value they will add to both the user and your organization.

Hyperlinks also add both effect and affect to a Web presentation. They can improve the *effect* by making additional content available to enhance the presentation's message. For example, a Web page providing instructions on how to put together a model airplane might be linked to a page that demonstrates common mistakes in making the model. Hyperlinks can improve *affect* through creative design, engaging the user's attention and/or senses more fully. In the case of the model airplane, diagrams, still photos, and/or videos of correct and incorrect procedures would enhance affect.

At the end of intersite hyperlink selection, the list of URLs to be linked to each page of a Web site is ready to be evaluated.

GO to...

http://www.travelocity.com
an American Airlines site that hyperlinks dozens of information sources for each city on its service route. Travel services include car rental and hotel reservation services. Weather reports, local hyperlinks, and other information sources are also available.

Linkage Evaluation

Once hyperlinks—intrapage, intrasite, and/or intersite—have been analyzed and identified for possible inclusion in the Web presentation, they need to be evaluated to ensure their benefits. Possible problems are too few, too many, or mismatched hyperlinks, or hyperlinks that somehow change the chunking of information in the presentation.

The problem of too few or too many links can be evaluated by using a linkage matrix like that shown in Figure 6-4. The linkage matrix, like the object relationship matrix introduced in Chapter 4, is set up in spreadsheet fashion. To create a linkage matrix, rows and columns are labeled with the names of each page and/or atomic information object in the home site, plus the names of the free hyperlinks to other sites. In Figure 6-4, only two entries, "Home" and "Selection," refer to individual pages. The other entries, for "Author," "Title," and so on, exist for every restaurant entry (in other words, the information for a single book is an atomic information object). The cells show **going** (G) and/or **returning** (R) links for each page. As in the object relationship matrix, the column and row headings are identical.

The ratio of links to the total possible should be in the 40-60% range. For the 11 Web column and row entries in Figure 6-4, the total number of possible links is 121 (11 × 11). Of these 121 possible links, 21, or 17%, are going links and 33, or 27%, are returning links, for 45% overall. If the overall percentage of links is above 60%, there are probably too many links; if it is below 40%, there are probably too few. But keep in mind that all rules are broken occasionally. If a site you are evaluating does break this rule, make sure there is a good reason for it.

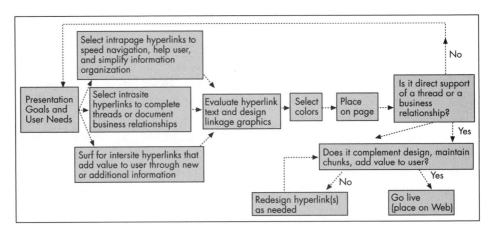

Figure 6-3 Rationale for selecting hyperlinks

Too Few Hyperlinks

Having too few intrapage hyperlinks is usually not a problem if each Web page has fewer than 150 lines of text. If pages have more, intrapage hyperlinks should be created to link every 10 to 20 lines of text.

Too few intrasite hyperlinks can imply that the number of user groups is low or that user actions are narrowly defined. A low percentage might also mean that return links should be increased to facilitate site maneuvering. Every page should provide for return to its parent page and to the site home page.

Having too few free hyperlinks reduces the usefulness of pages by depriving visitors of information that might add to their knowledge of the topic. By definition, reduced usefulness leads to fewer users, fewer sales, and fewer closures (or start-to-finish searches through your Web presentation's pages).

There is also the option of having no free hyperlinks, which can state the exclusivity of the site. Although free hyperlinks are often viewed positively by those on each end of the link, there are situations in which free hyperlinks might cause legal, political, or other business headaches that can be avoided by not using them.

Too Many Hyperlinks

Users confronted with too many hyperlinks become overwhelmed by the amount of information and tend to leave the presentation. Information overload is avoided by attending to the 7 ± 2 rule and the seven-second rule. Recall from Chapter 4 that the 7 ± 2 rule says that people, on average, can retain around seven chunks of information at a time, with a range of two either way. It's best not to expect Web page users to retain more than seven or so pieces of information in their head at once. This rule applied to linkages means that there should seldom be more than seven hyperlinks on any page. This rule applies to

Origins / Destinations	Home	Location Selection	Address	Map	Directions	Restaurant Select	Restaurant Address	Restaurant Map	Restaurant Directions	Restaurant Menu	Restaurant Page
Home	✕										
Location Selection	G/R	G/R									
Address	/R	G/R	✕								
Map	/R	/R	G/R	✕							
Directions	/R	/R	G/R	G/R	✕						
Restaurant Select	G/R	G/R	G/	G/	G/	G/R					
Restaurant Address		/R				/R	G/R				
Restaurant Map	/R	/R				/R	G/R	✕			
Restaurant Directions	/R	/R				/R	G/R	G/R	✕		
Restaurant Menu	/R	/R				/R	G/R	G/R	G/R	✕	
Restaurant Page						G/				G/	✕

G = Go to this page/site   R = Return from this page/site

Figure 6-4   Linkage matrix

both intrasite and intersite hyperlinks. Intrapage links are not bound by these constraints. Since intrapage links are introduced specifically to reduce information overload, they can be used almost at will.

Exceptions to the 7 ± 2 rule are based on detailed understanding of users' motivations and expectations when they come to the page. Examples of Web pages that violate the 7 ± 2 rule include search engines, sites that offer software download capabilities, and information providers that have long lists of items such that each entry goes to another Web page. The seven-second rule says that the amount of time a surfer will look at a page before deciding to go elsewhere is, on average, seven seconds. If a new surfer finds nothing of interest on a particular Web page in under seven seconds, the page may have too much information, too many hyperlinks, or both. In any case, this situation is easily fixed through page redesign and reduction in the number of hyperlinks. Again, depending on the information type, there are exceptions to this rule. The key is to match information and its format to intended users' needs.

Another situation that may lose users is a page with all hyperlinks. Every Web page should provide users with some useful information that takes them farther along a thread and reinforces their commitment to the Web presentation.

Mismatched Hyperlinks

Mismatched intrapage hyperlinks might occur if the link identifiers at the top of a Web page do not match the categories of the page contents. This problem can be avoided by carefully attending to the categories of information when creating intrapage links.

Mismatched intrasite hyperlinks can occur when links between site pages do not relate to either user needs or business relationships. Using only these criteria to create links will avoid the problem.

Poor selection of intersite hyperlinks may result in a mismatch between the goals of your presentation and the free link's presentation. This can lead to ambiguous interpretation of your presentation by a potential user. Further, those viewers interested in becoming users might pass over your organization's presentation for one that has a unified, single, consistent message. Free hyperlinks to whimsical sites that are solely designed for entertainment, for example, might attract surfers but send a mixed message about the seriousness of purpose for the page and its presenting organization.

Suppose you are an entrepreneurially-minded college student starting your own Web consulting company. You want your Web pages to project an image of your company as innovative, business oriented, and reliable. You build your Web pages, with daily updates, using innovative techniques, such as electronic Post-it notes, as shown in Figure 6-5. (An electronic Post-it note is a hyperlink that uses the image of this familiar slip of paper to highlight information. Clicking on the link brings the user to the information.) Several threads demonstrate different techniques of page design, different color selections, and so on. These pages have free hyperlinks to other Web presentations that also use innovative techniques.

So far, your pages are meeting your goals. But what if the main contents of the free link sites are the life and times of P. T. Barnum and Howard Stern—two people whom many consider to be shameless self-promoters? How do these links influence the message of your pages? The message is mixed, and that is a problem. On one hand, the innovativeness of design comes across as intended; on the other hand, your business message may now present you, too, as a shameless—possibly obnoxious—self-promoter who, like P. T. Barnum, believes "There's a sucker born every minute." Furthermore, links to these sites may divert your users' attention to *their* content. At best, the result of this mismatch between your site's goal and those of the free links is an ambiguous interpretation. Again, surfers who want to be users will probably turn to a site that has a clear, consistent message.

Impact of Hyperlinks on Chunking

Intrapage hyperlinks are designed to simplify access to voluminous text by chunking it into some category and by providing category-driven, on-page links. Therefore, assuming category selection that adds value for a given user group, intrapage hyperlinks will positively increase a Web page's usability. The more intuitive the category, the greater the usability.

Intrasite hyperlink design concentrates on providing user threads and linking business-related information objects. When these goals are firmly pursued, the effect of intrasite links is a natural flow of information and easy navigation. When those goals are not uniformly pursued, the effects on the user may be information overload, disorientation, and frustration. At best the outcome will be complaints, at worst it will be lost users.

Intersite hyperlinks can alter the way Web users chunk information by altering user perceptions of the home site. This problem is difficult to anticipate but can be identified during Web page testing by showing two groups different sets of pages and having them identify the threads. One group would evaluate Web pages without free links, the other the same pages with free links. If both groups identify the same threads, the links should be OK.

Postevaluation

After evaluation, the information structure diagram should be updated to reflect intrasite and intersite links. There is no way to do this for intrapage links. This documentation provides a complete picture of the Web site for the people who will be maintaining the site, and for new designers who need to familiarize themselves with the project. The product of linkage analysis and evaluation is a list of URLs to be added to the Web pages.

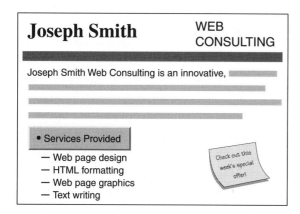

Figure 6-5   Electronic Post-it note

Linkage Composition Guidelines

Linkage composition is the writing of text to identify each link. This is an important activity since it determines, to some extent, the appeal of your site to users. Beyond the home page, users want to know "Where's the meat?" The "meat" is defined through hyperlink text and the few, well-chosen words that appear on the page.

Several general rules apply to hyperlink phrasing:

1. Use as few words as possible.
2. Be direct.
3. Make sure the words chosen accurately reflect the linked-to information object.
4. Make sure the words chosen accurately reflect the desired image of the organization.

The process of settling on the phrasing, or word content, of hyperlinks relies on information stewards' knowledge and understanding of their particular topic area. In the text analysis stage (Chapter 4), the essence of each information object was identified and documented with its other information. During hyperlink composition, that information provides the basis of hyperlink text. But, as the sites in Figure 6-6 show, information objects with the same essential characteristics might be presented differently on different Web presentations, depending on which aspect of the sponsoring organization is being emphasized.

Figure 6-6 shows the home pages of firms that provide electronic commerce security. These companies are in the same business, but their choice and presentation of hyperlinks send different messages to the potential user. The Xcert site has the fewest links but provides enough words for users to decide which link to use. Its message suggests that visitors already know about the company and are primarily interested in its products: various kinds of security software. The VeriSign site has about 30 links on its home page, with none in the first screen leading to its products. Its message focuses on promoting the company itself, as opposed to particular products. Finally, CertCo advertises its banking connection in large, bold type (the small print reveals it to be a spin-off of Bankers Trust) to establish its credibility. Its links to terminology and industry definitions differentiate it from the other two sites. By not assuming that viewers are already informed about Internet security issues and solutions, it is appealing to the broadest audience.

After the hyperlink text is written, the links are incorporated into the Web pages via *anchor* tags in HTML (see the CD-ROM for a full explanation). Text and link colors can be reevaluated at this time. Finally, all links and text are again evaluated to ensure that chunking and intention remain as intended.

Linkage Color Guidelines

Linkage color tells the user what is available and where he or she has been during a Web session. A **Web session** begins when the browser software, such as Netscape, is initiated and ends when it is closed. The color of hyperlink text is decided by the designer. Although each browser has its own default settings, these settings go into effect only if the designer has not specified link colors. If defined, the designer's colors override those specified by the browser.

Focus on products

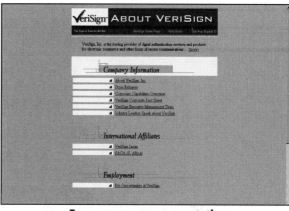

Focus on company reputation

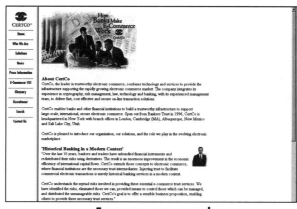

Focus on user appeal

Figure 6-6   Sites with similar content but different presentations

Each link can be in one of three states: available, active, or accessed. **Available hyperlinks** are those which have not been used in the current Web session. **Active hyperlinks** are those which have been clicked while the Web page is still in the process of loading. **Accessed hyperlinks** are those which have been accessed (the Web page has been completely loaded) during the current Web browser session. Each change in status is signified by a change in color. Available links become active links when clicked. Active links become accessed links when the Web page being sought is fully displayed.

Many sites that use a gray background also use browser defaults for all colors so as not to confuse the user. When using custom-colored links, it's important to make sure that each of the three colors assigned to indicate link status remains the same regardless of the color(s) selected for the page background. Users depend on consistent color cues to inform them about their status regarding each and every link. Good color design for hyperlink display, like good link design (or thread design), simplifies page structure and content by providing visual cues.

Linkage Summary

The placement, phrasing, and color of Web page links *should all work together toward the same end:* the user's easy, intuitive, exact access to the site's information and its overall goal. The following guidelines have these ends in mind:

- Hyperlinks should relate to one or more specific user groups and therefore to one or more specific threads through the Web presentation.

- Hyperlinks should be composed of simple, clearly written text that identifies jump locations.

- Link colors should contrast with other page elements so they are clearly distinguishable as hyperlinks.

- Hyperlinks for as many as nine (7 ± 2) other destinations from a single Web page can enhance the probability of closure for a user. This rule of thumb can be overridden for long lists of hyperlinks.

- Hyperlinks should be treated as a repetitive design element and be designed consistently.

- Intersite hyperlinks must be carefully and continually monitored. Web sites change all the time; a site once viewed as appropriate can become inappropriate in a day.

- No intersite hyperlinks should be used without careful evaluation of all the pages in the site. Unintended access to sites with information inappropriate in content or tone (effect or affect) to your presentation can result in embarrassment and even the loss of a user.

W e b   D e s i g n   i n   t h e   R e a l   W o r l d

Best Personalized Books

The group began defining hyperlinks with intrapage hyperlinks. Several pages had the potential for intrapage hyperlinks: the FAQ page, the newsletter page, and the page listing the books and their story lines. The group decided to use intrapage hyperlinks for the FAQ page and include both the questions and their answers on a single Web page. Users might want to browse other questions while answering a specific one, and this seemed to be the standard format for such pages. The format is *standard* because

the answer to each question is limited in length; maintaining a separate page for each answer would be tedious and difficult. The intrapage hyperlinks solved a potential maintenance problem while enhancing the usefulness of the site.

There were four published newsletters ready to go on the Web presentation. The group decided not to link them on a single page. Each edition of the newsletter would have its own page, and each edition would be listed on a menu page with its date and contents. The reason for this was that it would be easier to maintain each issue of the newsletter separately. When an issue or some of the information in it became obsolete, one or the other could easily be removed.

There were about 40 entries for the book covers and story lines—enough to warrant intrapage links. The problem was deciding how to categorize the books and how much extra space might be used in listing the categories. Alphabetizing didn't make sense, since alphabetical links wouldn't help a user who didn't know the title of the book. Subject matter was difficult to categorize, too. There were some categories—holiday books, general books, Disney books, sports books—but not all of the books could be categorized in a meaningful way. That idea was rejected. In the end, the group decided not to use intrapage links for this page since they could not agree on a short, meaningful way to index its contents.

Second, intrasite hyperlinks were defined. Once the threads had been defined by the group, Sue analyzed each thread and its related information objects to define the intrasite hyperlinks that matched the threads. The pages were already linked based on the business relationships established during creation of the text prototype. The threads were defined from the information structure diagram and the original definition of the activities each user group was expected to want. These hyperlinks were defined by the lines drawn earlier to connect information objects on the information structure diagram.

Finally, intersite hyperlinks were analyzed. There were several possibilities for these hyperlinks based on the global nature and licensing type of business Best pursued.

One was hyperlinks to U.S. government agencies, such as the Department of Commerce, to assist non-Americans in deciding whether to work with an American company. The Kalishers viewed this as too ambitious for the first presentation implementation, so that idea was abandoned.

Another possibility was intersite links to competitor pages to showcase the differences in quality of presentation and, therefore, the superior quality of Best products. But, wisely, Jack did not want to advertise his competitors' products.

Finally, the team considered free hyperlinks to sites maintained by Best licensees, so that single book buyers could choose a Best licensee directly, or to other sites that might inspire potential licensees to purchase a license. Jack felt that hyperlinks to individual licensees would be a mistake in that Best would then be offering extra support to those few licensees with Web sites. The benefit of providing single book sales and giving the sales to a distributor near the buyer would be lost or, worse, licensees without Web sites might become angry enough over the preferential treatment to end their agreement with Best.

Similarly, other sites that might inspire a licensee had drawbacks. Any subtle or overt coercion would be grounds for canceling an agreement. For instance, a site might discuss

6 CHAPTER

how easy and highly profitable it can be to operate a home-based business. If someone purchased a license thinking they might make lots of money with little work, they could end up suing Best for false advertising. This would be bad for Best's reputation and would defeat the purpose of the site. Also, sites on the importance of reading and so on were changeable at the whim of the owners. The content of these sites was beyond the Kalishers' control; they didn't want to risk sending users to a site that had changed without their knowledge. Therefore, no free hyperlinks were used in the Best page design.

For the actual phrasing of the hyperlinks the team wanted simple, "folksy" English that would be unambiguous without sounding "stuffy." Phrasing for hyperlinks was decided by taking each business function or concept and coming up with a simple alternative to describe it for the Web pages. Sue and Wendy then rephrased these descriptions; they decided that active verbs and simple questions provided the informality and clarity they wanted. Figure 6-7 shows the business

functions, categorized by type of user, and their matching wording on Best's home page.

The colors were left to Sue's discretion. She chose a shade of blue for available hyperlinks that was close to the turquoise color used in the Best logo and most of its advertising. This color became a repetitive element, visually connecting the hyperlinks to the turquoise Best header at the top and the Best address and contact information at the bottom of each page. Wendy asked about the possibility of using a multicolored border for each page to further link the site to Best's printed materials. It was decided not to use the border until Web technology matured a bit more. Borders would require specialized graphics that would take too long to load and would hinder users.

Accessed and active hyperlinks were defined as a light shade of purple that provided unmistakable contrast with the blue, yet was unobtrusive. The same shade was used for both because active link colors are displayed for only a brief time (while a Web page or URL is located and loaded).

User	Alternative	Phrasing
Book Buyer	Purchase a single book	Buy a book
Potential Licensee	How to become a licensee	Become a dealer
Potential/Current Licensees	Marketing	Marketing Best products
Potential/Current Licensees	Learning about the company	Who is Best?
Potential/Current Licensees	Current events	What's new at Best?
Current Licensees	Support & sales	Existing licensee support

Figure 6-7 Phrasing for home page hyperlinks

S u m m a r y

Three types of hyperlinks are available to Web site developers: intrapage, intrasite, and intersite. Intrapage hyperlinks facilitate single page navigation. Intrasite hyperlinks tie threads together and document business relationships between information objects. Intersite hyperlinks are a unique, value-adding feature of the Web that give users access to Web presentations outside your own. The purpose of all three types of hyperlinks is to add to the purpose and emotional appeal of your Web presentation pages.

Selection of hyperlinks is crucial to a successful set of pages, since the alternatives (too few, too many, or mismatched hyperlinks or hyperlinks that interfere with information chunking) are confusion, appeal to an unintended audience, information overload, or reduced usefulness. Selection should be based on how well the link supports the Web presentation's message and goals, its page appeal, the emotional tone, ease of use, and user needs. When all hyperlinks for a site have been selected, they are evaluated to verify that threads remain intact, business relationships are preserved, and value is added to the Web site. The product of linkage analysis and evaluation is a list of URLs and user-defined intrapage identifiers to be added to Web pages. Both information stewards and designers participate in linkage analysis and evaluation, with stewards making the final decision.

During linkage composition the specific hyperlink text is written and incorporated into the page. Finally, colors for available, active, and accessed hyperlinks are selected and implemented.

R e v i e w   Q u e s t i o n s

1. What is the difference between an intrasite link and an intersite link?
2. Discuss the statement "The more hyperlinks the better." Do you agree? Why or why not?
3. What are three advantages and disadvantages of using free hyperlinks?
4. What steps can you take to minimize the chances of making a poor link selection?
5. Who should participate in free link selection?
6. How frequently should intersite hyperlinks be reviewed for appropriateness to your site? Who should perform the review and why?
7. What is the distinction between link analysis and link composition?
8. What factors should a designer consider in defining hypertext colors?
9. When should bold colors, such as tangerine or lime, be used? When should muted colors, such as teal or dark green, be used?
10. What questions should be asked when reevaluating hyperlinks?

6 CHAPTER

P r o j e c t s

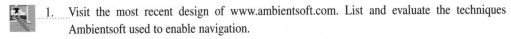

1. Visit the most recent design of www.ambientsoft.com. List and evaluate the techniques Ambientsoft used to enable navigation.

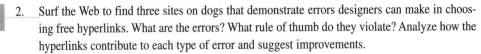

2. Surf the Web to find three sites on dogs that demonstrate errors designers can make in choosing free hyperlinks. What are the errors? What rule of thumb do they violate? Analyze how the hyperlinks contribute to each type of error and suggest improvements.

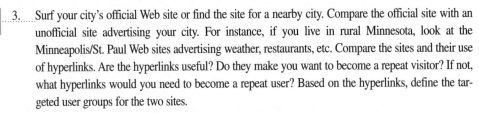

3. Surf your city's official Web site or find the site for a nearby city. Compare the official site with an unofficial site advertising your city. For instance, if you live in rural Minnesota, look at the Minneapolis/St. Paul Web sites advertising weather, restaurants, etc. Compare the sites and their use of hyperlinks. Are the hyperlinks useful? Do they make you want to become a repeat visitor? If not, what hyperlinks would you need to become a repeat user? Based on the hyperlinks, define the targeted user groups for the two sites.

C a s e   P r o j e c t

1. Drawing on your information object diagram, prepare a linkage matrix showing the linkages you plan to implement to enable viewers to navigate intuitively and easily through the pages. Based on an analysis of hyperlinks that go to and return from each page, ensure that all threads and business relationships are covered.

2. Select the specific colors for hypertext for your hyperlinks. Incorporate them into your Web project pages. Defend your choices.

3. Select and define intersite hyperlinks to enhance the effect and affect of the pages. Define the user group(s) and the added value they will receive from each link.

F u r t h e r   R e a d i n g

- *Inside the Internet.* http://www.cobb.com/int
- *Internet World.* http://www.iw.com
- *Internet Magazine.* http://www.zdimag.com
- *Web Techniques.* http://www.webtechniques.com
- Carter, R. C. "Visual Search with Color." *Journal of Experimental Psychology Human Perception and Performance.* 8 (1982): 127-136.
- Christ, R. E. "Review and Analysis of Color Coding Research for Visual Displays." *Human Factors.* 17 (1975): 542-570.
- Kristof, Ray, and Amy Satran. *Interactivity by Design.* Mountain View, Calif.: Adobe Press, 1995.
- Landrow, George P. *Hypertext: The Convergence of Contemporary Critical Theory and Technology.* Baltimore: Johns Hopkins University Press, 1992.

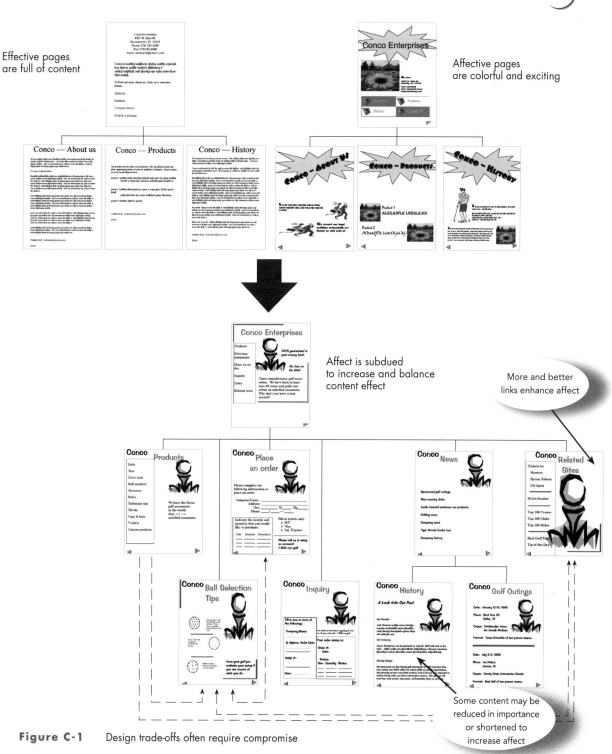

Effective pages
are full of content

Affective pages
are colorful and exciting

Affect is subdued
to increase and balance
content effect

More and better
links enhance affect

Some content may be
reduced in importance
or shortened to
increase affect

Figure C-1   Design trade-offs often require compromise

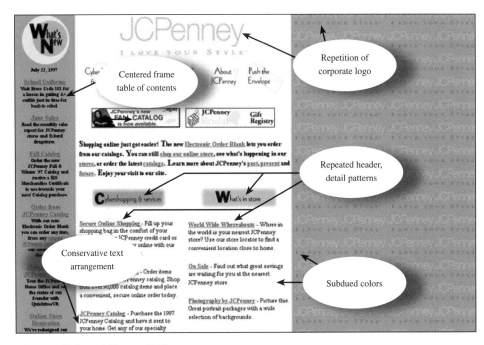

Figure C-2   JCPenney Web site

Figure C-3   Neiman Marcus Web site

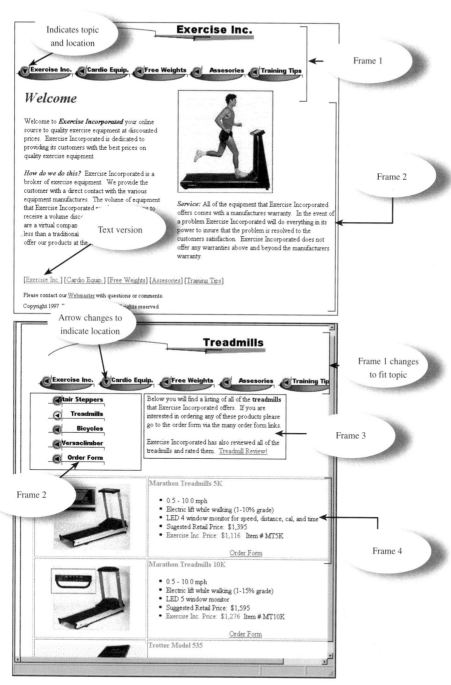

Figure C-4   Frame format shows topic and user location

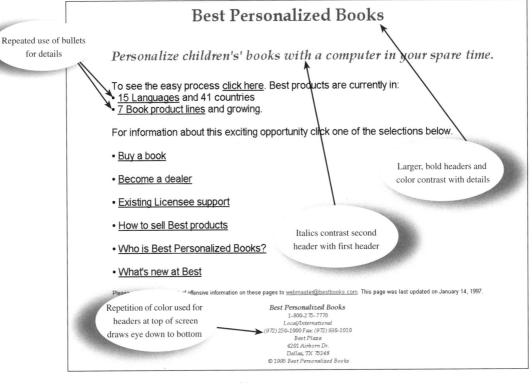

Repeated use of bullets for details

Best Personalized Books

Personalize children's' books with a computer in your spare time.

To see the easy process click here. Best products are currently in:
15 Languages and 41 countries
• 7 Book product lines and growing.

For information about this exciting opportunity click one of the selections below.

• Buy a book

• Become a dealer

• Existing Licensee support

• How to sell Best products

• Who is Best Personalized Books?

• What's new at Best

Larger, bold headers and color contrast with details

Italics contrast second header with first header

Plea... ...offensive information on these pages to webmaster@bestbooks.com. This page was last updated on January 14, 1997.

Repetition of color used for headers at top of screen draws eye down to bottom

Best Personalized Books
1-800-275-7770
Local/International
(972) 250-1000 Fax: (972) 930-1010
Best Plaza
4201 Airborn Dr.
Dallas, TX 75248
© 1995 Best Personalized Books

Figure C-5   Early text version of home page

Figure C-6   Universal icons

Figure C-7   Varying photo effects

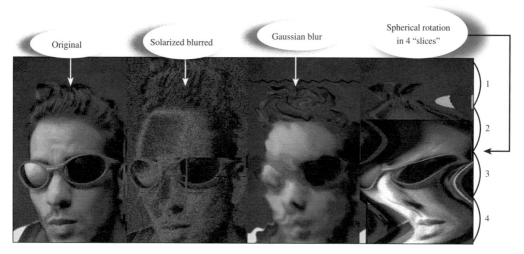

Figure C-8   Photo distortions

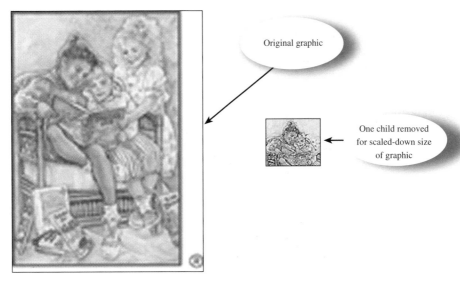

Figure C-9 Graphic chosen for hyperlinks

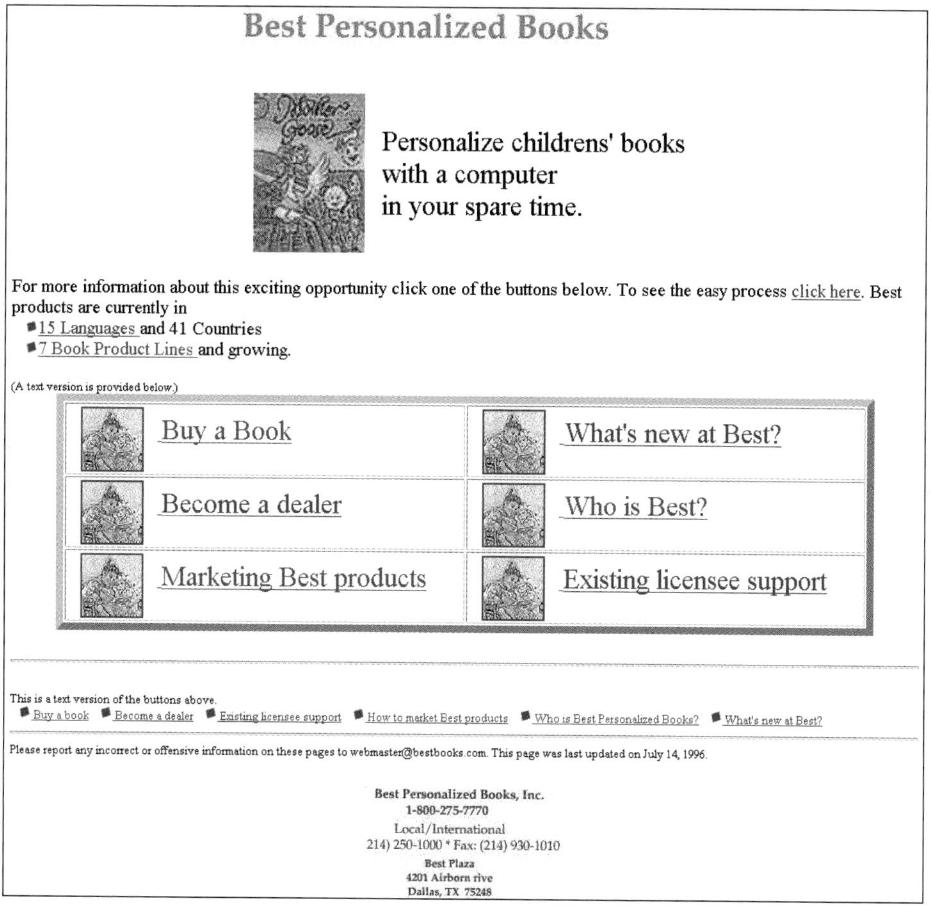

Best Personalized Books

Personalize childrens' books
with a computer
in your spare time.

For more information about this exciting opportunity click one of the buttons below. To see the easy process click here. Best products are currently in
- 15 Languages and 41 Countries
- 7 Book Product Lines and growing.

(A text version is provided below.)

Buy a Book		What's new at Best?
Become a dealer		Who is Best?
Marketing Best products		Existing licensee support

This is a text version of the buttons above.
- Buy a book - Become a dealer - Existing licensee support - How to market Best products - Who is Best Personalized Books? - What's new at Best?

Please report any incorrect or offensive information on these pages to webmaster@bestbooks.com. This page was last updated on July 14, 1996.

Best Personalized Books, Inc.
1-800-275-7770
Local/International
214) 250-1000 * Fax: (214) 930-1010
Best Plaza
4201 Airborn rive
Dallas, TX 75248

Figure C-10   Best home page

Figure C-11   Best marketing support page

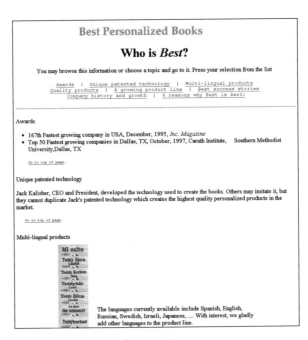

Figure C-12   "Who is Best?" page

7

Multimedia Analysis
and Composition

In This Chapter You Will Learn To:

- Identify the general types of multimedia now available
- Explain the four purposes multimedia generally serve on a Web site: description, decoration, exploration, and demonstration
- Explain the best use of a specific multimedia format
- Match purpose and format to achieve the optimum affect, effect, and navigational efficiency
- Assess the impact of each multimedia selection on the layout of each page and make necessary adjustments
- Evaluate the collective impact of the multimedia on the tone and content of the entire Web presentation

W e b   D e s i g n   i n   t h e   R e a l   W o r l d

Best Personalized Books

Some of Best's goals for its Web presentation were addressed by the use of multimedia. These goals were:

1. To demonstrate the simplicity of the book production process

2. To appeal to individual book buyers and potential licensees

3. To complete threads for book purchasing by individual book buyers, licensee ordering, and inquiring by all users

4. To increase Web site attractiveness while not compromising effect

Multimedia: An Overview

Most organizations implement several generations of Web presentations. In fact, there is a definite maturation process that takes place during the development and deployment of successive generations of Web presentations, as the organization learns more about its users and how the site is utilized. For that reason, many organizations deliberately choose to implement multimedia in stages. Frequently, text-only pages are formatted and prototyped first. Then, simple multimedia are added, such as graphics, icons, diagrams, charts, maps, and so on. More complex technologies, particularly audio and video, may or may not be implemented depending on their appropriateness, cost, and the growth in number of visits. Repeat users want more and better Web content. These desires translate into providing new threads that increase user capabilities and enhance design so as to better inform (say, by demonstration rather than text), better entertain (by animation rather than still cartoons), and better persuade (by opportunity to enter orders in addition to inquiring about them).

When discussed as they apply to Web presentations—and for the purposes of this book—**multimedia** consist of text, graphics, sound, animation, and video or other media combined into a single product or presentation. Print, for example, is a single medium, as is audio. Computer interfaces or hypermedia programs that integrate two or more different media, however, produce multimedia.

Multimedia for Web presentations are available in a diverse, ever-changing set of software products. Figure 7-1 lists a selection of these ever-expanding products by medium. Keep them in mind for your presentation as you read about the process of integrating multimedia into Web pages.

Medium	Representative products
Graphics, icons, drawings, cartoons	gif Converter, Photoshop, CorelDraw, Stylist, Adobe Illustrator, Freehand, Shockwave, Object Dancer, Debabelizer, Chromatica, Paint Alchemy, Terrazzo, Expression Poser, Detailer, Adobe After Effects
Photos, plain, distorted, or otherwise	Photoshop, Extensis, Eye Candy, Pantone Color Controls, 3D Café
Geographic maps	GIS Software, Photoshop
Time lines, time-oriented diagrams, Venn diagrams	Many drawing packages, Adobe Type Reunion, Type on Call
Flow charts, organization charts	Flowcharter, Visio, many drawing packages
Spreadsheets, bar charts, pie charts, line charts	Excel, Formula1, Lotus 1-2-3, Toolbook
Video	Director, Authorware, QuickTime, Active Movie, Firewire, Broadway, Toolbook
Audio	Real Audio, Waves, Sound Forge, Sound Canvas, Synauthor, Liquid Audio
Telephone connection*	NetPhone, FreeTel, Cool Talk, Web Phone, Web Talk, DigiPhone, Internet Phone, Televox
E-mail	Netscape Navigator, Internet Explorer, many e-mail packages
Forms, applications, applets, scripts	CGI/Perl, Java, JavaScript, Visual Basic, VB Script, Shockwave, Vivo Active, Café, J++, Toolbook, ActiveX
Animation	VRML, CGI/Perl, Java, JavaScript, Visual Basic

Note: See the section "Determine the Format of Enhancements" for definitions and examples of most of the media types listed in the chart.

Telephone connection refers to products that provide telephone-type services directly over the Internet.

Figure 7-1   Multimedia software products

The overall look and feel of the presentation is a key concern throughout each generation of its development. Because multimedia influence both page and whole presentation affect more than any other single design component, the guidelines in this section relate largely to developing affective presentations. However, by using multimedia to improve the *affect* of a presentation, it is also possible to increase the accuracy and completeness of the content, that is, its *effect*. Sensible use of multimedia can also improve navigational efficiency. Multimedia can sometimes convey information with more clarity than plain text (as in a video demonstration, versus a text description, of changing a tire) and with more efficiency (a picture can be worth a thousand words). Multimedia also make it possible to present several alternatives to a given course of action at once. (For instance, a video of an appendectomy might show several acceptable methods of incision and removal.)

Use of multimedia does not mean throwing away the text version of your presentation. Remember that users throughout the world still use low-grade computers[1] and that many telecommunications systems and modems cannot readily accommodate graphical representation of Web pages. You should produce two versions of your presentation. A high-tech, multimedia version should be produced to define you and your organization as innovative and leading edge, while a low-tech, text-only version should be produced for those who cannot accommodate the high-tech version.

Because both high-tech and low-tech versions of the pages are needed, you might hold off on the implementation of multimedia until there is a clear indication of its usefulness to your site (based on user feedback, new content, etc.). At the rate technology changes, any kind of multimedia you implement today may be obsolete tomorrow. Delaying the introduction of sophisticated multimedia may not be detrimental to an organization's image. Many organizations begin with a presentation consisting of text and simple charts or line drawings or photos and then add sound, video, or animation later. How quickly they move to full-fledged multimedia depends on what their competitors are doing and the nature of their business. Entertainment and graphic arts companies, for instance, often begin with a high level of multimedia.

The main goal of using multimedia in a Web presentation is to increase its affect by communicating as much information as possible as succinctly as possible, that is, with the fewest possible words, images, and so forth. One example is the use of a chart to replace a table of numbers. Pie charts, bar charts, time lines, and the like can convey more meaning more concisely and precisely than long strings of numbers. Multimedia can also be used, for example, to demonstrate—in a series of images—the operation of a mechanical device that would be hard to describe in text. And, as the award-winning Berk site listed shows, not all multimedia need to be business oriented to be useful.

GO to...   **http://www.Berk.com/highview/mtr/tree.htm** to see an interactive applet (that is, a small self-contained program) that lets you test your reflexes in a drag race. This site downloads two ActiveX components to your machine. ActiveX is a Microsoft product that provides Web interactivity. (Berk won an ActiveX demonstration competition with this site.)

Deciding what types of multimedia are most appropriate for a Web presentation occurs during **multimedia analysis**. During this analysis, the purpose of a potential nontext presentation of each information object should be clearly identified and tested for compliance with both the desired visual affect and overall project goal(s). The product of multimedia analysis is a list of potential multimedia selections to be deployed on the site.

During **multimedia composition**, the actual multimedia to be used are selected and, if necessary, created and then inserted into the Web presentation. Once multimedia have been selected, they may be either developed from existing material (such as a photo already in the files) or created from scratch (drawings of new icons to serve as hypertext links). Creating some complex objects requires hiring specialists.

1. The Intel 386-generation PC in much use around the world is slower than 100MHz, usually under 16MB RAM, and cannot accommodate large graphics, any audio, or any video.

Introducing each medium to the presentation, whether an icon or an audio recording, is its own small Web project. The more complex the technology, the more elaborate and specialized the talents of the designers. Each medium is worthy of, and has, books devoted to the creation of information objects. (See suggestions for further reading at the end of the chapter.) For instance, creating an audio recording requires a script, HTML presentation or other component, recording software, adjustment of recorded sounds for bass, middle, and treble tones, physical compaction and storage for Web access, and creation of a hyperlink on a Web page. The hyperlink creation can be performed by someone with a modest amount of HTML training (and is within the scope of this text), whereas recording and sound engineering would be performed by a Webmaster or other technical specialist. Specific instruction for creating multimedia objects is thus largely beyond the scope of this chapter. However, guidelines on the physical layout of Web pages, once the multimedia are in hand, are covered in this chapter.

The product of multimedia analysis and composition is a complete, up-to-date, multimedia Web presentation. If the presentation has not already been implemented in its text version or in stages as multimedia objects were implemented, at the end of this composition phase, it is ready to go live on the World Wide Web.

Key Roles

As in the other analysis stages of Web design, the information stewards and designers share multimedia analysis work. In this phase, the designers guide the work by outlining the technologies available and helping to establish a priority for developing them.

During multimedia composition, the designers implement the various selected multimedia objects. Most designers do not have all of the skills needed to create all possible kinds of multimedia objects. Depending on the type of multimedia, designers may need to hire audio engineers, video directors, actors, writers, lighting experts, cartoonists, photographers, cartographers, and so on to supplement their own skills. These additional resources require management, and this can be the responsibility of either the designers or the information stewards. The designers, though, are involved in the actual computer implementation, regardless of the medium. As with all other aspects of a Web presentation, the information stewards approve the final products for implementation on the Web.

Multimedia Analysis Guidelines

During multimedia analysis, each information object and each page in the Web presentation is examined to determine what useful purpose might be served by replacing, supplementing, or otherwise enhancing the object or page with multimedia. The "best," or most appropriate, medium for each targeted object and page is then identified. The best medium for a particular object or page might be chosen from those immediately available or those that need to be created. The degree to which multimedia objects can be created is often determined by time and money constraints. Money for purchasing or renting hardware, software, and media specialists should be traded off with the benefits to be gained from the multimedia.

The steps in multimedia analysis are as follows:

1. Determine the purpose of enhancements.

2. Determine the format of enhancements.

3. Match purpose and format to select multimedia for development.

Determine the Purpose of Enhancements

The purpose of multimedia depends on user needs and capabilities (both technical and nontechnical). The less usage-literate the user groups, the more likely multimedia would help them to visualize and understand the presentation. In analyzing information objects as potential targets for multimedia application, you should think in terms of what purpose they will serve for the user. Generally, multimedia serve one of the following purposes: description, decoration, exploration, or demonstration.

Description can be a depiction, narration, presentation of events, or portrayal of some object. Descriptive multimedia elements serve the purpose of improving on or clarifying the meaning of information conveyed in the original text. For example, an annotated drawing of a subway or museum can show points of interest and convey other information that a text-only description could not do in the same amount of space or time. Figure 7-2 includes both a picture and a written description of a computer mouse. If you were asked to draw a mouse based on the text description, without having ever seen one before, chances are your sketch would not look like the real thing.

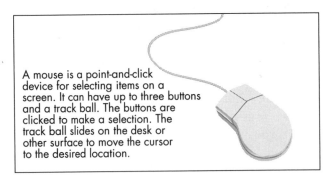

A mouse is a point-and-click device for selecting items on a screen. It can have up to three buttons and a track ball. The buttons are clicked to make a selection. The track ball slides on the desk or other surface to move the cursor to the desired location.

Figure 7-2   Picture versus written description

Decoration is an adornment or other beautifying graphic that is not strictly required for meeting the goals of the presentation. Decoration can contribute to the tone of a presentation (the Peapod site contains cartoon bags of groceries, suggesting that shopping this way can be fun), provide visual repetition (a break line on a page that is composed of graphical elements, such as Christmas tree lights to support a holiday theme), or highlight a focal point (a background that is shaded such that the color lightens as it nears the focal point).

Figure 7-3 shows multimedia decorations for an elementary school page. The decorations—school building, books with apple, and blackboard—provide no additional information but help to give the impression of a grade school and set a friendly tone.

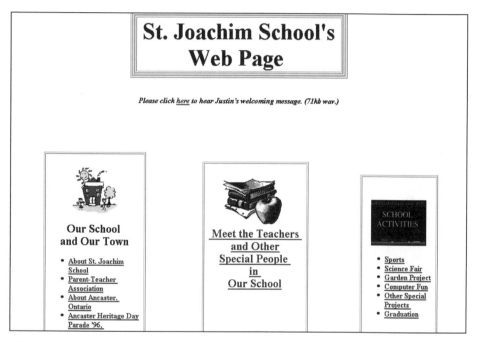

Figure 7-3   Multimedia decorations

Exploration is the interactive, user-controlled unfolding of a thread. The user is free to choose among the objects presented for viewing such that he or she controls the experience. Exploration may use graphics, animation, and/or video to present the user with a self-selected sequence of "events." Digital Equipment Corporation's Web site makes exploration available to users by allowing them to configure a computer system onscreen. Virtually every user is given the opportunity to define a unique configuration based on his or her specific needs. Another example of exploratory

GO to...

http://www.digital.com
to try DEC's software that
allows exploration of equipment
configuration alternatives.

GO to...

http://www.idsoftware.com
and play id Software's
games Doom and Quake for
examples of exploration.

multimedia can be found in id Software's games Doom and Quake, in which the Web site user adopts a persona and plays an adventure game.

Designers use exploration techniques to help viewers experience something that is active, dynamic, or composed of a sequence of events best performed at their own pace and under their own control. Exploration is best used in situations in which the user defines the context or requirements that best fit his or her needs (as in DEC's site), or when there is *no one best way* and the user's entertainment and engagement are increased by self-determined context and events (as in id Software's games).

Whereas exploration involves the *user*-controlled unfolding of a thread, **demonstration** involves the *designer*-controlled unfolding of a thread. Like exploration, demonstration might use graphics, animation, and/or video to present the user with a certain sequence of "events." A good candidate for demonstration would be a sequence of dance steps on a site hosted by an organization that teaches ballroom dancing. The difference between this demonstration and an exploration is that the user makes no further choice after clicking on the link that connects to the demonstration; it unfolds automatically each time a user accesses it. Demonstrations are used when the user groups share a common set of needs or when there is a clear *right* way to perform the activity.

Determine the Format of Enhancements

More than 20 different types of multimedia are currently available to convey information (see Figure 7-1). In this section, we highlight the most common types of multimedia currently used in business Web presentations. Although each is discussed separately, it is important to note that when more than one is used they should work together with the text and with each other to form an integrated, consistent whole.

The visual effect produced by the combination of lines, light, shade, and color should be consistent with the attitude or state of feeling created by the words and phrasing of the text. This is what is meant by establishing a consistent tone or mood in a Web presentation. A Web page's tone has an immediate subliminal effect; that is, it makes an impression below the viewer's threshold of conscious awareness. Subliminal messages enhance the affect of the direct message (the page content).

Icons are easily recognized "buttons" or symbolic depictions of an idea, event, or subject. The best icons are intuitive, universal, scaleable (that is, they work at any size), and simple. These goals are not easily achieved; the more abstract the idea, the more difficult it is to portray its essence in a single symbol. Figure C-6 (see color insert) shows a number of universal icons.

GO to...

http://www.kodak.com
to see how Kodak uses photos to demonstrate the quality
of its products.

Photos, drawings, and cartoons increase presentation affect by making it feel more personal, and all of these techniques are inexpensive. In fact, their low cost sometimes causes Web designers to overuse them. Anytime affect is added, its value must be weighed against any resulting loss of effect. Also because of their low cost, these media are useful substitutes for video presentations. For instance, a sequence of photos, drawings, or cartoons can often depict the steps in a process, such as changing a tire, just as well as a video can.

Photos can give a face to quoted words, lending credibility and making the material less abstract. Photo tours of a university, for example, might sell a prospective student by giving him or her a more intimate look at its campus. Various treatments of photos and other images can be used to influence tone. The sharp edges on photos can be taken off and their appearance softened and integrated into text through use of a torn-page fragment frame. (See Figure C-7 in the color insert.) Distortions such as stretched or strangely colored images can all enhance visual affect. (See Figure C-8 in the color insert.) The left-most photo in the set is untouched. The second shows an overexposed "sunburn" effect that might be used to add interest to a discussion of global warming or the health risks associated with sunburn or to inject humor into a discussion of how to deal with stress. The third photo distorts, or "stretches," the features and could be paired with the untouched photo to highlight a discussion of mental growth and development. The right-most picture has been given a wavy effect and might be used to add humor to a discussion of motion sickness.

Do not, in general, use photos of individual people unless the face can be plainly seen. As a rule, individuals (and just about anything else) are better represented in a drawing or cartoon if only poor-quality photos are available.

Cartoons are particularly good for presenting socially taboo subjects in a way that does not offend. They can also convey friendliness. A series of cartoons demonstrating the consequences of "halitosis" might be a more humorous way for a breath mint company to present its case. Cartoons must be in keeping with the overall tone of the site. Use of a silly cartoon in a site filled with serious prose or other unexpected combinations of words and images will confuse viewers.

Animation, audio, and video draw users into a presentation by introducing movement and/or sound. Whereas audio and video are used to capture real or staged events, animation is used to create events. In animation, **transitions**—identifying, depicting, and moving between each major condition or status—and **integration**—seeing the effect of the entire segment and not only each frame—are important design issues.

Audio and video, especially, personalize the presentation by providing a sense of person-to-person connection. Text can be replaced with an audio or video recording of a specific individual, making the message much more personal. Using CU-SeeMe (freeware from Cornell University that allows users on different PCs to talk to and see each other or to show each other screen contents) and small cameras, the New Jersey Institute of Technology and other schools teach courses to distant students. Using CU-SeeMe, for example, a student at a remote site can ask a question directly of the instructor and the instructor can answer that question while both can see and talk to each other.

Selection of animation, video, and sometimes audio often stems from a need to convey some sequence of events with emphasis on specific actions. For football games, the Sports Zone site, and the sites of most TV networks use animation to show game progress and status. The Sports Zone

GO to...

http://www.sportszone.com
and http://www.sportsline.com
to compare styles for live interviews,
play-by-play calls, and other interesting audio and animated information.

GO to...

http://www.eai.com/
to test the downloadable animations from Engineering Animation.
A leader in computer-generated
animation, the company's work
ranges from simulating the birth of
the universe in the "Big Bang" to
providing 3D coloring software for
children.

GO to...

http://www.paris.org/Musees/Louvre
(note the uppercase characters) to
see the famous museum's exhibits.

GO to...

http://www.virtualproperties.com
or http://www.southseasplantation.
com/ssp_movs.html for video tours
of real estate property.

uses a grid with a dot to show ball position while an audio narrator describes the play. The university photo tour mentioned above might be enhanced by an audio description of the more interesting campus walkways and buildings, or by sound bites from a typical class-room. News sites often enhance an article by adding video clips of the people involved in the story.

Video and audio are best used for live-action events. Texas A&M University builds a bonfire at homecoming every year and provides updates on the progress of the building and burning every 15 minutes. A wide variety of things have been displayed on the Web. People put images of babies, fish, animals, cities, and even coffee pots on their Web sites and update them every few min-utes or even seconds with a new, "live" image.

Video can provide multiple perspectives of a fixed object. (As can multiple still photos or drawings—and less expensively.) Visit a museum, such as the Louvre, and see its exhibits. Wander through a home in one of the many real estate sites on the Web.

Video, audio, and animation are useful in instructional "how-to" courses, and they can also be used to demon-strate the functioning of an object such as a machine. They can also be used to demonstrate an activity that is not eas-ily described in words.

As with photos, the quality of the audio or video used is important. The power of video is substantial, but it can be easily wasted if its content is of poor quality. Similarly, no audio is better than poor audio.

The presentation of complex and voluminous numeric information is simplified by **tables** and **charts** that summarize the data. Tables present rows and columns of information—either alphabetic or numeric—in a familiar spreadsheet format. The table in Figure 7-4 contains data on the number of pounds of five different kinds of fabric (silk, cotton, polyester, wool, microfiber) that might be sold by a textile manufacturer during each of the first six months of the year.

Charts can be used to emphasize certain characteristics or trends that can be found in the data. Each type of chart has its optimal uses. The charts in Figures 7-5 to 7-7 emphasize different trends that can be found in the data in Figure 7-4.

	January	February	March	April	May	June
Silk	10000	8000	8000	5000	5000	5000
Cotton	5000	6000	6000	7500	8000	9000
Polyester	7500	7500	7000	7500	7000	7500
Wool	12000	10000	5000	2000	4000	17000
Microfiber	22000	24000	23000	12000	10000	10000

Figure 7-4   Pounds of fabric sold per month

Bar charts are composed of a horizontal axis (the x-axis) and a vertical axis (the y-axis). One of these axes has a measurement scale on which two or more bars are plotted. Plotting the bars against the horizontal scale creates a horizontal bar chart. Plotting them against the vertical scale creates a vertical bar chart (as shown in Figure 7-5). Both are used to show quantitative comparisons between two or more items of interest. Figure 7-5, for instance, makes it easier to see the relative amounts of silk, cotton, polyester, wool, and microfiber sold during each of the first six months of the year.

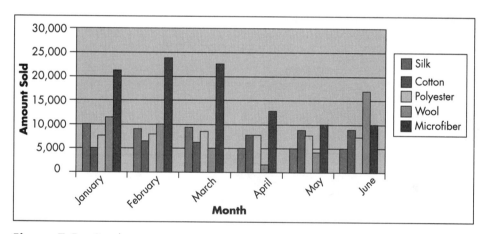

Figure 7-5   Bar chart

The scale for all kinds of charts should always be shown plainly. (Figure 7-5 clearly shows the scale in months on the x-axis and in pounds of fabric on the y-axis.) Always explain complex charts and tables in accompanying text. Give them titles that will help the user interpret the information without restating obvious facts from the chart or table.

A **pie chart**, a circle divided into pie-shaped parts, demonstrates the relationship of a whole to its parts and the parts to each other. The pie chart in Figure 7-6a is a good example of how to use a pie chart. It shows the contribution (in pounds) to sales for a single month, that is, the parts of total sales in relation to each other. The chart in Figure 7-6b is a poor example of a pie chart. This example shows, for a single type of fiber (silk), its percent of total sales for five months. Such information would be more meaningful if presented alongside the same information for the other four fiber types, but a pie chart doesn't lend itself to this kind of depiction. A line chart, such as that in Figure 7-7, can be used to illustrate this kind of comparison.

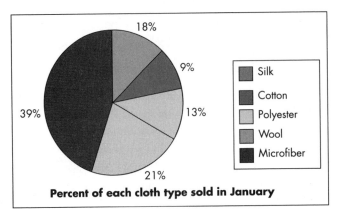

Figure 7-6a   Good use of pie chart

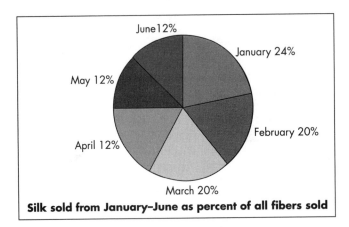

Figure 7-6b   Poor use of pie chart

A **line chart** is best used to depict changes or trends over time, relationships, and comparisons. Figure 7-7, for instance, allows for easy comparison of the sales trends for each of the five fabric types for the first six months of the year.

Other fairly straightforward and useful kinds of charts and diagrams include the organization chart, the flow chart, the time line, the time-oriented diagram, and the Venn diagram.

An **organization chart** is used to depict the structure of a group and is typically used by firms to indicate the relationship of its various departments and the people within them. Because this kind of chart also usually indicates lines of authority (what person or what department reports to another), it can also be called a hierarchical chart. See Figure 7-8 for an example.

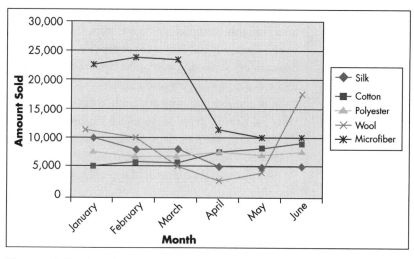

Figure 7-7   Line chart

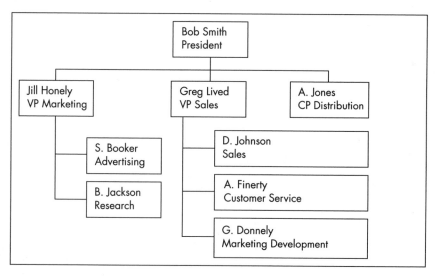

Figure 7-8   Organization chart

A **flow chart** emphasizes sequence. It shows how a series of activities, procedures, operations, events, ideas, or other aspects of a system are related to each other. Words or symbols can be used to indicate the specific elements of the process, and arrows are used to indicate the direction of the flow between them. Figure 7-9 contains a flow chart of an individual's morning routine.

GO to... | http://www.pbs.org/wgbh/
pages/nova/
to see examples of time lines
that display historical information. You can also go to
the special effects pages at
http://www.pbs.org/
wgbh/pages/specialfx/
sfxhome.html.

Time lines are often used to depict a sequence of related events as they occurred over time: days, weeks, months, years—almost any unit of time can be depicted. The significant battles in the course of a war, or the significant events in the course of a human life, are good examples.

In a time-oriented diagram, each column represents a "slice" of time. Each row identifies the location or activity at that time. In Figure 7-10, the rows show location and topic for a multitrack conference. Time-oriented diagrams are best used for depicting several dimensions of a specific "slice" of time.

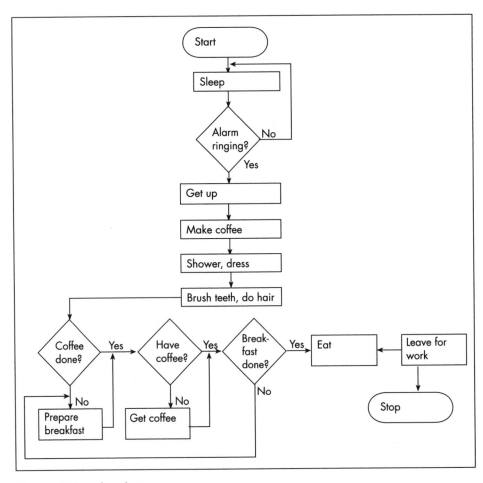

Figure 7-9 Flow chart

Room	SA	SB	SD	SE	MA	MC	MD	ME	TA
	8:45-10:15	10:30-12	2:45-4:15	4:30-6	8-9:30	1-2:30	2:45-4:15	4:30-6	6-9:2
Reunion B	OR/MS Applications				Railroad Applications				
Reunion C	Airline Tutorials								
Cascade B									
Reunion E							Aviation Applications		
Reunion F							Military Applications		
Reunion G							Decision Analysis		
Reunion H							Education		
Regency A							Manufacturing & Service Opertions		
Regency B	Manufacturing & Service Operations Management							Inventory M	
Regency C	Flexible Mfg.		OR Apps. in Semiconductor Mfg.				P & C		
Cascade A	Transportation Science					Facilities Location			
Cascade B								Transportation Scienc	
Cotton Bowl	Railroad Applications			Supply Chain Operations					
Colonnade F1									
Sanford					New Product Development				
Colonnade 1	Technology Transfer			Finance				Envir	
Bryan A								Technology	
Bryan B		Organizational Science							
Latimer A	Health Applications							Health Car	
Latimer B	DEA & Productivity					Quality Mgmt.		Ser	
Duncan A	Special Events					Electronic Commerc			
Duncan B	Information Systems				State-of-the-Art in IS				
Brisbane A						Management of Medical Tec			
Dealey	Workshops				Teacher Program				
Executive	Logistics/Supply Chains							Decis	
Directors		Finance	Econ.		Marketing				M
Colonnade A	Statistics & Reliability								
Latimer A									
Colonnade B	Student Affairs				Applied Probability				
Latimer B									
Colonnade C	Interface Between AI/OR			Artificial Intelligence		AI/OR Techniques in Proj			

Figure 7-10   Time-oriented diagram

A **Venn diagram** can be used to show the relationship between things or groups of things. It consists of separate or overlapping circles. In a Venn diagram of three circles, each represents an information category. For example, one circle could represent a group of things that are "tall," another a group of things that are "heavy," and another a group of things that are "round." The space where all three circles overlap represents yet a fourth group of things: those that are tall, heavy, and round. See Figure 7-11.

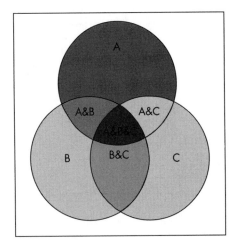

Figure 7-11   Venn diagram

Forms, applications, scripts, and **applets** allow interactions between users and the organization sponsoring the Web presentation. **Forms** are fill-in-the-blank screens that users complete to ask questions, request information, or otherwise communicate with a Web presenter. An **application** is functional software that supports some business function, such as checking a database or processing a transaction. **Applets** and **scripts** are functions written in Web-customized languages, such as VB Script or Java. Applets can provide interaction, "live" animation (as in the game Doom), simple data display, and update processing.

Both applications and applets provide access to descriptive information. They can access business data, summarizing or condensing it into charts, graphs, or spreadsheets or presenting it in some other user-friendly way. Both require coordination between traditional MIS and Web designers. The coordination is needed to ensure that that information supplied for the Web is stored in a location and format that make it accessible and usable for both MIS and Web needs.

Match Purpose and Format

The table in Figure 7-12 lists the various multimedia formats available to choose from, along with the purposes each is best capable of fulfilling. All formats can be used to add description to your Web presentation, but to achieve decoration, exploration, or demonstration, you must be more selective.

Format/Medium	Purpose			
	Description	**Decoration**	**Exploration**	**Demonstration**
Animation	✓	✓	✓	✓
Audio	✓	✓	✓	✓
Bar charts	✓			
Cartoons	✓	✓	Several in a sequence	Several in a sequence
Color (e.g., shaded boxes, backgrounds)	✓	✓		
Computer applications, applets, scripts	✓		✓	✓
E-mail	✓		✓	✓
Flow charts	✓			
Forms	✓		✓	✓
Geographic maps	✓	✓		
Icons	✓			
Line charts	✓	✓		
Organization charts	✓	✓		
Photos, distorted or otherwise touched up	✓	✓		
Photos, plain	✓	✓	Several in a sequence	Several in a sequence
Pie charts	✓			
Spreadsheets	✓	✓		
Telephone connection	✓		✓	✓
Timelines, time-oriented diagrams	✓	✓	✓	✓
Venn diagrams	✓			
Video	✓		✓	✓

Figure 7-12   Multimedia formats and purposes

The goal in matching purpose and format is the same as for all other Web design activities—to meet the three criteria for a successful presentation: affectiveness, effectiveness, and navigational efficiency. Since some forms of multimedia can cost so much to develop, another criterion to seriously consider is cost effectiveness. You want to spend the least amount of money necessary to obtain the best possible outcome for the Web presentation.

Each type of multimedia can add to a site's **affectiveness** if its content and tone, or style, are in sync with the overall content and emotional tone of the presentation. To accomplish this, there must be a good fit between each information object and the multimedia format selected for it. For instance, a video on how to change a tire is more appropriate to a tire company's site than a funky, distorted photo of a tire. A demonstration video portrays the tire company as helpful; a distorted photo of a tire merely portrays the company as "different."

An **effective** multimedia selection is one that adds to the accuracy and completeness of the presentation. Tables and charts usually fit this description for quantitative information. If misused, or unwisely selected, however, multimedia can just as effectively hide or distort the meaning behind the numbers. Icons, cartoons, and other types of drawings can add effect by providing an easily understood summary of otherwise indigestible text. Audio and video might also enhance effect by providing an otherwise doubtable presentation with realism and validity. Nearly all types of the media can add to effect by distilling voluminous text into a shortened form.

Navigational efficiency is also a consideration in multimedia selection. Efficiency, in this discussion, relates primarily to the load time of a page. The more complex and closer to reality the medium, the more digital capacity it consumes and, hence, the more time it takes to transmit the page, store it on a server, and process it. If the process takes too much time, users are bound to become impatient and leave the site.

While there are no hard rules as to how much time is too much time, a rule of thumb used by many organizations is that no single page should require the loading of more than 100K of materials. Text files, unless very large, are usually under 20K. A 2-inch-$\times$ 2-inch photo is about 65K. So, to stay below 100K, the text HTML can have one photo plus four to six icons. Some organizations place a lower limit on their home page to keep its load time under seven seconds (about 25K). Even a brief audio recording or video clip at present requires more than 1MB (or 1,000K), but there are design techniques that can camouflage delays. Technology is now available that will "push" 5 to 10

GO to...

http://www.amazon.com a huge Internet book store and buy a book, or visit http://www.elibrary.com, an electronic library, and sign up for its services free for the first month. Both sites have registration and sales forms. Visit http://java.sun.com/applets/index.html for links to other sites, for forms, and for Java applets that can be downloaded. Visit http://www.travelocity.com, the American Airlines site, for interactive selection of travel itineraries and purchase of airline tickets, reservation of hotel rooms, and booking of rental cars.

seconds of sound or video at a time. While you watch one "slice" of information, the next slice is being downloaded.

As the purpose and format of the multimedia to be used are selected, the choices can be identified with notations on the prototype. As each information object is checked off, the multimedia choice should be reevaluated to make sure that the information object—not the multimedia object associated with it—remains the focus of the page. For instance, a video on how to enter an order might distract a buyer long enough for him to lose interest in the purchase.

To summarize, during multimedia analysis, the focus is largely on determining the purpose and format of each multimedia object on the page. Each information object is assessed to determine how it might benefit from being replaced by or supplemented with a multimedia object. You might choose to replace bullets in a list with an icon, or to supplement a text table with a chart.

Multimedia Composition Guidelines

Picking up where multimedia analysis leaves off, multimedia composition involves:

1. Selecting or developing the actual multimedia objects to be integrated in the Web presentation

2. Integrating those objects on each page

3. Evaluating the total effect of the newly implemented objects on the overall presentation

Assessment of the overall impact of the multimedia on the presentation will probably result in changes; their collective impact must be weighed against their individual contributions to the site. You may elect not to replace a certain element in all locations to maintain contrast between objects. Or you may elect to replace the element in all locations to ensure repetition. Decoration can add to a presentation's appeal, but it is easily overdone; care must be taken to evaluate the cumulative affect of any decorative graphics. As with every stage of Web design, the whole is just as important as its parts. The presentation, as a whole, should look like the same person designed the entire set of pages. It should have a unified look and feel.

Reviewing the layout of each page in terms of multimedia object placement involves evaluating contrast, proximity, repetition, and alignment. A multimedia reference is one of two types: an immediate presentation or a hyperlink. The immediate presentation media include anything that is stored in a graphic format, such as icons, photos, cartoons, charts, and so on. These are presented as an integral part of a Web page; that is, they are visible when the page is loaded to the browser. Other media, including audio, video, and nonhypertext files such as word processing and spreadsheet files, are integrated as hyperlinks, which, when clicked, are activated and viewed. Both types of page entries must be reviewed to ensure that the look and feel of the pages remain as planned and that no individual entry is more prominent than it is meant to be.

Similarly, the collective impact of multimedia objects is evaluated for the site as a whole. The evaluation phase includes people outside the design team and should include intended users. They are asked to evaluate the complete design, pointing out any items that do not "fit" or that overpower other items. Hyperlinked media are all tested and evaluated by the group for their value added, appropriateness to the presentation, and design quality.

There is a point at which too much repetition leads to a boring, even confusing sameness that is ultimately off-putting to users. Repetition becomes overwhelming primarily in the use of opening graphics for pages that include an icon or photo along with descriptive text for the page. If page after page repeats the same icon, such as the "tucows" icon in Figure 7-13, the users may lose their sense of location in the site. If all the pages look pretty much alike, users may feel like they've never left the home page.

Figure 7-13 Overuse of repetition

Visual maps are excellent indicators of location, but they can take a lot of time to develop. Visual maps that subtly show directions are effective and unobtrusive (see Figure 7-14). A home page map might show a diagram that becomes highlighted with movement through the site. A second-level page would show the related box on the diagram as highlighted and the home page dimmed. Icons in the form of arrows can also be used to show direction.

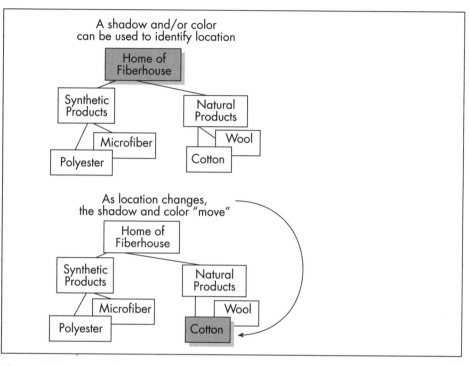

A shadow and/or color
can be used to identify location

As location changes,
the shadow and color "move"

Figure 7-14   Visual maps

 W e b   D e s i g n   i n   t h e   R e a l   W o r l d

Best Personalized Books

Best Personalized Books is sophisticated in its marketing approach, using interesting and informative graphics in its marketing materials. So rather than develop new multimedia for the Web, Jack and Wendy decided to use as many existing graphics as possible. By using the graphics, photos, and various icons that were familiar to current licensees, they hoped to provide repetition in all of the company's marketing efforts.

(Note: There was no analysis of multimedia possibilities for intersite links because Jack and Wendy had decided not to use them.)

The topic of icons or graphics to accompany the hyperlink text was discussed first. One choice was to use a different book cover as adornment for each hyperlink. This was not a good idea because viewers might study the graphics to determine their relationship to the text rather than click on the text for more information. Instead, the team selected a graphic used in much of Best's advertising, showing several children reading a book. The graphic was modified to remove one child and maintain fidelity of the images when shrunk to a half-inch square icon (see Figure C-9 in the color insert). This choice provided repetition and would, the team hoped, clearly signal a hyperlink. In addition, showing children reading might reinforce the idea that children will increase time with personalized books.

Four photos demonstrating the process of making a book (see Figure 3-9) were copied with their accompanying text. The text was left-justified, with the photos placed against the left margin. This placement proved to be unexciting when the team evaluated the prototype, and was revised. In the final design, the text and photos alternated left- and right-justified placement, with the first showing text-photo, the second photo-text, and so on.

Icons for all book products were reproduced and used on the "Best Product Information" page. This form of decoration enhanced the information by showing the quality and intricacy of each book cover's design. The title and a brief description of the story line accompanied each cover. On this Web page there were 17 book covers shown on the left, with text on the right. This arrangement would avoid confusing the reader with too many left-to-right eye movements. It would be easy for a user to find a specific title. On testing the page, the Best staff thought it was too long and required too much scrolling. The book cover icons and the text were retained, but the page was

redesigned to put the list in two columns, thus halving the scrolling time and providing faster access to the information.

The team consciously selected graphics from current marketing materials for use on every Web page. The goal was for these adornments to enhance the image of Best by showing it as an innovative, creative, successful, assertive company that was at the top of its field. Several examples show how the Best image was enhanced through graphics:

- Instead of using only plain text to describe multilingual products, the team decided to demonstrate the "Teddy Bear" book cover in 15 languages.

- In the section on "Quality of Products," photos of licensees and their testimonials were used to increase the emphasis on this information and to personalize it.

- Selected testimonials augmented marketing information by showing quotes with photos of the licensees praising a product or sales technique.

- To confirm information on "Best Success Stories," a digitized version of a letter from President Clinton was shown. The letter congratulates Jack for *Inc. Magazine*'s recognition of his company's growth.

Three pages of the Best Web site are shown here to demonstrate its use of color, layout, and graphics (see Figures C-10 through C-12 in the color insert). The home page uses the graphic of the girls in each table menu entry for repetition, and to tie the Web site to Best's print advertising. The Best mar- keting support page uses a graphic of an advertising display to reinforce the topic. The "Who is Best?" page summarizes the history and successes of the company. When the pages first display, they are easy to read, although almost all pages require some scrolling to see all of the information.

S u m m a r y

Multimedia can enhance the affect, effect, and navigational efficiency of a Web presentation and can reduce the number of words required to express an idea. Opportunities to replace or supplement existing text with multimedia are identified during multimedia analysis. The steps in this analysis are to define the purpose of multimedia enhancements, determine their format, and match purpose and format with the goals of affectiveness, effectiveness, and efficiency in mind.

The basic purposes of multimedia enhancements are description, decoration, exploration, or demonstration. Descriptive multimedia narrate events or portray some object. They help to clarify the message of the information object. Decorations are not intended to clarify information but to contribute to visual repetition, tone, or emphasis of a focal point. Decorations are usually fun but can be easily overdone. Exploration and demonstration are used in the unfolding of a thread by the user and presenter, respectively. In the Best case, the four photos depicting the process of creating a customized book are examples of demonstration.

Alternatives to text-only presentations include a variety of media, including audio, video, drawings, cartoons, photos, charts, and tables. In the selection of multimedia for a particular information object, load time for the item must be considered along with the technical potential of the using audience to access the multimedia object. The rule of thumb used by many organizations is that a single Web page should require no more than 100K of information.

During multimedia composition, the multimedia objects selected are obtained from existing material or created from scratch. They are then integrated into each page, either as direct-display objects, such as a graphic or photo, or as indirect hyperlinked objects, such as a video clip. The layout of each page is then reviewed to account for the addition of multimedia, and the entire Web presentation is reevaluated to assess the collective impact of the multimedia.

CHAPTER 7

R e v i e w   Q u e s t i o n s

1. When is the use of multimedia justified? What purposes can be served by incorporating multimedia into a Web presentation?

2. What factors should be taken into account when choosing the format of multimedia?

3. In what ways do multimedia influence or contribute to affectiveness, effectiveness, and navigational efficiency?

4. What is an applet? How might one be used?

5. Give an example of how each of the following multimedia formats might be used: bar chart, pie chart, line chart, animation.

6. List several appropriate uses of a time-oriented diagram.

7. There is no perfect design. Consequently, the implementation of multimedia requires trade-offs. What kind of trade-offs are required when choosing between, say, an audio recording and text? Between video, cartoons, and photos?

8. What is a frequent mistake made by designers when using decoration?

9. Discuss the statement "A Web site's pages should look as if they were designed by one person." What does this statement mean? Why is it important? How is it accomplished?

10. A mortuary wants to establish a mood of calmness and peace on its Web presentation. What forms of multimedia would be appropriate? How should they be used? A rock band wants to let people know how upbeat and modern its music is. What multimedia should it consider? Why?

P r o j e c t s

 1. Surf the Web and find a presentation you really enjoy. Drawing on the guidelines in this chapter, critique the use of three or four multimedia devices individually and as a whole. What individual purpose does each device serve? How does each contribute or detract from the emotional tone of the site? Summarize aspects of the presentation that illustrate good composition.

 2. Surf the Web to find a site that makes excellent use of multimedia to convey information better than a text presentation could. Discuss why the multimedia enhances the information. Identify a Web site that fails to use multimedia effectively. Explain why it fails, basing your argument on the ideas presented in this chapter. Suggest five specific improvements to the presentation.

 3. Surf the Web to find sites that use one or more of each of the following: bar chart, pie chart, line chart, table, video, audio, animation, and cartoons. Evaluate each site and rate its effectiveness on use of multimedia. Rate each on a scale of 1 to 5 (least effective to most effective) and then defend your rating based on ideas presented in this chapter.

C a s e   P r o j e c t

1. Consider the text for each information object in your Web presentation. Could you convey the information more affectively, effectively, or efficiently with multimedia? Could you convey more information with multimedia? Evaluate the source materials of each information object to determine existing media that might be used. Consider implementing the desired multimedia and your expected users' capability to benefit from them. (Can they make use of high-end technology? Will use of such technology be important to them? What is to be gained from the richer information presentation?) Complete the Web design and implement it.

F u r t h e r   R e a d i n g

- Articles in *Inside the Internet, Internet World, Web Techniques, Internet Magazine.* Visit their associated Web sites: http://www.cobb.com/int, http://www.iw.com, http://www.Webtechniques.com, and http://www.zdimag.com

- Berk, Emily, and Joseph Devlin, eds. *Hypertext/Hypermedia Handbook.* New York: McGraw-Hill, 1991.

- Deep, John and Peter Holfelder. *Developing CGI Applications with Perl.* New York: John Wiley & Sons, 1996.

- Giordan, Daniel. *Kai's Magic Toolbox.* Indianapolis, Ind.: Hayden Books, 1996.

- Goodman, Danny. *Java Script Handbook.* Foster City, Calif.: IDG Books Worldwide, 1996.

- Johnson, Eric F. *Cross Platform Perl for Unix and Windows NT.* New York: M&T Books, 1996.

- Kristof, Ray, and Amy Satran. *Interactivity by Design.* Mountain View, Calif.: Adobe Press, 1995.

- Lang, Curt and Jeff Chow. *Database Publishing on the Web and Intranets.* Scottsdale, AZ: The Coriolis Group, Inc., 1996.

- McManus, Jeffrey P. *How to Program Visual Basic 5.* Emeryville, CA: Ziff-Davis Press, 1997.

- Morrison, Michael, et al. *Java 1.1.* Indianapolis, IN: Sams Net, Inc., 1997.

- Parker, Roger C. *One Minute Designer.* Indianapolis, Ind.: Que Corporation, 1993.

- Rabb, Margaret Y. *The Presentation Design Book,* 1st and 2d eds. Chapel Hill, N.C.: Ventana Press, 1990 and 1993.

- Thompson, Nigel. *3D Graphics Programming for Windows 95.* Redmond, Wash.: Microsoft Press, 1996.

- Tufte, Edward R. *Envisioning Information.* Cheshire, Conn.: Graphics Press, 1990.

7
CHAPTER

Part  4

ONGOING SUPPORT

No Web presentation is ever really finished. From the beginning, members of the Web presentation team should be planning for maintenance and improvement. The extent of the support a site will need once it's operational depends substantially on the "life" of the information on each page and on the information gained from earlier versions of the Web site. Some pages will require constant refreshing to be kept current. For example, online newspapers, such as *USA Today*, update their home page every hour. But all Web presentations should be monitored periodically to ensure that their content and design remain aligned with users' needs and with the company's activities and goals. Key considerations for an organization's continued support of its Web site are described in Chapter 8.

8

Maintenance and

Continuous Improvement

In This Chapter You Will Learn To:

- Identify the reasons for maintenance and continuous improvement of a Web site
- Identify the key roles involved in supporting a site
- List and explain the four basic activities involved in maintaining and improving a site
- Describe the strategies used for technology surveillance

W e b   D e s i g n   i n   t h e   R e a l   W o r l d

Best Personalized Books

Jack and Wendy's vision for the "look" of their Web site evolved over time. By the time this book was being printed, they had decided to eliminate the hypertext table menus. The new design would have two frames—one that showed hyperlinks, and one that showed all other information. (By the time you read this book, that design may have changed, too.)

Overview: Supporting a Web Site

Web presentations need constant monitoring, maintenance, and improvement for a variety of reasons:

1. All information has a limited life span of usefulness.

2. As information stewards and presenters gain experience over time, they will expand their vision of what can be done with the site.

3. Competitors and organizations against which an organization compares itself develop new Web presentations.

4. New technologies become available that allow upgrading of pages to increase affect or effect.

A site that is not upgraded in terms of look and technology, and not improved and updated in terms of content and navigational techniques, becomes dated and will experience reduced numbers of users. Just like the attractions at an amusement park, the features of a Web site must be constantly upgraded and improved if it is to keep drawing crowds. Companies must continuously upgrade to ensure effective, affective, and efficient Web presentations that reflect changes in the company, the way it conducts its business, and the audiences it serves via the Web.

Key Roles

To ensure the continued viability of its Web site, every organization requires key personnel whose job it is to keep it performing up to expectations. The more important the Web presentation is to the organization and its mission, the stronger the support should be.

Key personnel allocated to Web maintenance and support are presenters, information stewards, and designers. Presenters direct and fund continuing Web activities. They work with information stewards to determine a Web strategy and decide the extent of electronic commerce on the Web.

Information stewards and designers have much of the same areas of responsibility in the maintenance and improvement of the Web site that they did during its development. Stewards continue to be responsible for Web content and should monitor those pages relating to the business function for which they are responsible. Designers are responsible for implementing the changes recommended by the stewards and presenters. As in the development process, stewards and designers work as a team to perform these activities, cycling through the phases of analysis and design as required to accomplish their goal: an up-to-date, active Web presentation that meets the needs of their various user groups.

A new key role introduced once the site is on line is that of Webmaster. The term is applied to the operations manager—the person who keeps the Web site up and running. There may actually be several people who fill the role if coverage is needed 24 hours a day, seven days a week. The Webmaster is generally the primary user contact, and his or her e-mail address is posted on the site. One part of the job involves forwarding mail from users to the appropriate parties, such as customer service or sales. Other functions may include evaluating technologies beneficial to the Web site and recommending upgrades to phone service, operating systems, hardware, and software, as necessary.

Maintaining and Improving Content

The majority of work performed during maintenance of Web sites concerns content: upgrading, keeping current, and adding new information and functionality to the site. Identifying out-of-date, incorrect, misunderstood, or unintended use of content is crucial to a Web site's viability.

New information for existing Web-supported areas, new business areas for Web presentation, and new user groups might be identified by stewards as reasons to reexamine and/or expand the Web site. Changes in the organization itself are also cause for updating Web content. When the organization changes, stewards should review information on the Web to make sure it reflects the new company organization, products, services, and/or policies. A kind of warning system should be designed so that whenever a change takes place in the organization's business that also affects the information on the Web pages, relevant parties are notified so the appropriate changes can be made.

Knowing the volatility of each information object allows a schedule of maintenance to be established to ensure that no one object is out of date. The information objects should be sorted by volatility and a schedule set up to monitor the items on an hourly, daily, weekly, monthly, or annual schedule according to how rapidly they are likely to change. The checking is performed by stewards and Web designers.

Beyond fixing errors, coping with out-of-date information, and maintaining accurate organizational information, designers, stewards, and presenters must commit to an ongoing learning effort. They should ask themselves at least once a month, "Given what we know now, is the content of our pages meeting users' needs?" New developments in the organization or new discoveries about users will result in a "no" answer to this question. This is a cue to initiate changes in content.

Additional changes in content can be initiated by the external users. The more central the Web site is to the organization and its mission, the more important it is to solicit some type of external input about the effectiveness of its content. This can be accomplished through the use of focus groups, partial user group Web site usage, and/or formal questionnaire surveys. Each method has its strengths and weaknesses.

Focus Groups

The focus group method of content evaluation can be used with any type of user, ranging from the general public to specific user groups. Focus groups are designed to obtain information from potential users without directly asking for it. Potential users are invited to come to a designated site to participate in a focus group. They are told the purpose is to seek their opinion on World Wide Web sites. Then, when gathered together, each person is seated at a terminal and given the same task. It is important that the right task is picked to serve this purpose; if not, bad results might be the product of a poorly chosen task, not a poorly designed site. (For instance, if you wanted to test general buying behavior, you might put together an electronic mall of sites. The task assigned to the focus group would be a general one, such as buying a gift. A good outcome would be having satisfied buyers who found your site and used it to buy their gift.) The group starts from a "home" page that you have provided, which contains links to several Web sites, including yours. Your hope is that most of the group will visit and navigate your site, but you don't lead them there; you want them to discover the site on their own, guided only by the parameters of the assigned task.

The assignment has three possible results: the potential users won't go to your site at all; they go to the site but do not successfully navigate the pages; they go to the site and navigate it successfully, find the desired information, and complete the task. Three discussion groups are then organized on the basis of these three outcomes.

Those members of the focus group who did not go to your site are asked to discuss where they did go and why. If they completed the task without visiting your site, it is important to ask them how they did it. The feedback from this group is used to improve the marketing of the Web site to search engines or, perhaps, to change the wording of the Web pages to more closely reflect users' mental models.

Those in the second group, who visited your site but failed to complete the task, should be asked to explain their perception of the task and their reaction to the site relative to the task: From this you can obtain information leading to the redevelopment of threads and the redesign and/or rephrasing of page content to ensure that surfers perceive the usefulness of the site in achieving this task.

Those who completed the task successfully should first be asked to discuss their experience in general. You might say, for instance, "First I'd like you to describe your feelings and thoughts while you did this exercise. Let's start with the menu page. [Name of person], what did you do and why?" The goal is for each person to talk about what contributed to their decisions to go to each site and to each page within a site. The group provides feedback on all of the sites, based on their usefulness, value added, ease of navigation, intuitive feel, and the overall design. If their perception of the purpose of a link is not what you intended, you'll want to consider making some adjustments. Ideally, you should not ask questions specifically about your site unless there seems to be no other way to get the information. You want honest, unbiased responses from the group.

Depending on the success and failure rates of the group overall, the Web site could be deployed or redesigned. For generally successful groups, deployment would be reasonable. For completely unsuccessful groups, redesign would be prudent.

8

CHAPTER

In screening people for the focus group, keep in mind the needs of the user. For a site aimed at the general public, such as the site for a department store, the focus group can (and should) be drawn from the general public. For sites with a narrower range, focus group members should be drawn from the targeted user group. A site on a particular disease, say cataracts, would target a specific group of medical professionals and patients; it would not be likely to appeal to the average person or the average surfer.

Partial User Group Web Site Usage

A different technique that should return information similar to that supplied by focus groups is to deploy the Web site but not advertise it (for instance, do not place references on Yahoo or other search engines). A small group of intended users (such as selected customers) could be informed of the site's location and uses and allowed to access it. This group, being an intended user group, would be expected to make regular use of the site. Usage statistics and site navigation tracking would be collected to determine how often the site is visited and which threads are most used. After an initial usage period, the users could be asked, individually or collectively, how useful they found their experience, whether the site met their needs, and what criticisms or improvements they might suggest. This method is best used for Web sites designed to appeal to a specific user group, not one looking to attract the general public.

Questionnaire Surveys

Questionnaires are best used when a specific population of users is expected and targeted. They provide a way to ask large numbers of individuals their opinions in a voluntary, anonymous environment. Users can respond at their convenience rather than convening on a certain day at a certain time. The issue with questionnaires is how the information gained can be used.

If used with small groups, questionnaires can employ open- or closed-ended questions. (See Chapter 3.) The responses would have to be tallied by hand, and the cost in labor would be high. In addition, because it is small, the sample chosen would have to be selected carefully to be representative of the using population.

For large groups of respondents, questionnaires must necessarily use closed-ended questions. The questionnaires could be tallied by machine, and statistics could be run on the results to provide overall conclusions.

GO to... http//www.isworld.com and look for questionnaires on information technology topics.

Because of these two specific types of limitations—on sample size with the smaller groups, question type with the larger groups—questionnaires should be carefully constructed, with the phrasing and order of the questions tested to elicit useful information. Vague remarks (such as "I didn't like the design") will not help solve any problems that might be uncovered.

Maintaining and Improving Design

Some designs wear well with time, others do not. One or two months after a Web site becomes active (and about every month or so thereafter) it is a good idea for each development team member to review the site afresh. Each individual should try to imagine that he or she is visiting the Web site for the first time. They should ask themselves the following questions:

- Do my eyes travel naturally to the focal point of the site?
- Is the design inviting?
- Are the threads running through the site relevant and complete?
- Do the pages work together gracefully and function as an integrated whole?

A negative response to any of these questions indicates the need to consider redesign.

The team should also keep up with changes in the design of sites sponsored by competing organizations, organizations in the same industry, or organizations whose Web presentations and practices are admired. If any of these parties has changed their design approach, you may want to consider doing the same. Webmasters should monitor Web sites, user groups (through chat groups and bulletin boards), and so on to stay current on bugs found, fixes available, and new releases of software.

Surveys, interviews, and other forms of user feedback, while more difficult to conduct on affectiveness issues than on content, are nevertheless excellent sources of cues for redesign. In general, the more important affectiveness attributes such as fashion and style are to your organization, the more frequently your design should be reviewed and, probably, the more frequently Web pages—at least the home and other key pages—should be redesigned.

Part of upgrading the design means taking advantage of maturing technologies likely to increase the site's affectiveness. (Methods of finding out about these technologies, often called technology surveillance, will be discussed shortly.)

Maintaining and Improving Linkages

Anytime you review the content or design of your pages, click every hyperlink to make sure each still works. Follow several threads to assess the naturalness, ease, and efficiency of navigation. User feedback and Web use statistics are indicators of the frequency of thread use. During the early stages of design there is a tendency to treat all threads equally. Experience generally shows that users travel down some threads more often than others. Frequently followed threads should be made as efficient as possible. Anytime a change is made in the content or in the page design, the results should be examined for their effect on the efficiency of the existing linkages.

Intrapage links should be evaluated periodically as new information is added to the site. For each atomic information object added, a new link is also added as necessary.

Interpage links are maintained by tracking usage of the pages and the threads between pages. The Webmaster and designer develop programs to do such tracking, using the statistics on users and their activities available from the server. The designers analyze the usage statistics and summarize the information for the stewards. Then the maintenance team develops new or revised threads based on actual Web page usage. This analysis might also lead to Web page content changes. If the statistics show that some kinds of information are used more than others, the less used pages might be redesigned and/or discontinued. The highly used pages might be upgraded with improved design to continually entice users.

CHAPTER 8

Intersite links should be visited at least once a week. The more vital a link is to the purposes of a page, the more often it should be visited to ensure that the information there is still consistent with Web page objectives. In general, the more volatile the information at the end of a free link, the more frequently it should be reviewed.

In general, the more intrasite or intersite linkages you have, the more frequently the linkages should be reviewed.

Maintaining and Improving Technology

In addition to content, design, and linkages, a Web site's overall performance depends on the technology platform (that is, the computer and its software) on which it is implemented. Web technology changes constantly and rapidly. Web design and content originally considered problematic or too expensive may become practicable.

As a rule, the greater the complexity of the content and the more advanced the technology, the more constant and important technology surveillance and site upgrading becomes. **Technology surveillance** involves the ongoing observation and evaluation of new technologies from the time they are announced until they mature enough to use. The purpose of technology surveillance is to determine whether or not using the new technology will improve the existing system's performance or better achieve the site's overall objectives.

Surveillance includes reading magazines, visiting E-zines (electronic magazines), attending trade shows, talking with vendors, and discussing developments with people in other organizations. This investigation is conducted to identify new technologies that might be appropriate for your site.

Since some aspects of technology surveillance require technical knowledge, part of this task is usually conducted by the Webmaster. Nevertheless, designers and stewards should participate as well. The technical people know the limits and requirements of the technology itself, while the stewards and designers (as well as anyone else providing creative services, such as artists or advertising experts) can envision how to exploit the technology and leverage its benefits across multiple user groups.

Surveillance can be both active and passive. **Active surveillance** is the search for a new technology directed by the desire to solve a specific problem with or add a new dimension to the Web site. **Passive surveillance** involves the occasional observation of trends, competitors' activities, new technologies, and the like that *may* be of significance to the organization.

Active surveillance activities are initiated through one of several processes. Someone in the company may recognize a need that cannot be served by existing technology. In this case, the surveillance group initiates a project to analyze the problem, define the requirements of a solution, then locate alternative technologies to solve the problem. Once technologies are identified, the alternatives are researched and reduced to a small number, usually three or fewer, for further research and actual trial. The technology that performs the best during the trial procedure is selected for negotiation of contracts and eventual deployment. A model of active surveillance is presented in Figure 8-1.

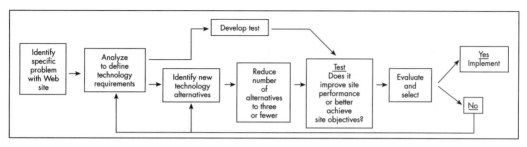

Figure 8-1   Model of active surveillance

Periodically, the group or person charged with active surveillance surveys the company's internal user community to determine which technologies they envision as becoming useful for their area of responsibility. This practice can take several forms. It may involve simply asking those in the user community to list new technologies they want to see put under surveillance, or it may involve employing complex methods of analysis. One such method, the **Delphi method**, involves developing and then circulating to all users questionnaires on the estimated importance of emerging technologies. The responses are analyzed to determine how respondents have ranked the importance of each technology. Reassessments, reranking, and resurveying are then performed as needed until a consensus is reached on which technologies will be assessed in coming months.

Passive surveillance is an occasional activity. It can be as simple as surfing the Web to identify the technologies being used at innovative sites. Passive surveillance also includes reading magazines or visiting electronic magazines, visiting trade shows, and talking to vendors, all in an effort to monitor new technologies that might be appropriate and useful. All of these techniques are actually a subset of those used in active surveillance. The difference is that passive surveillance entails looking for technologies without having a specific problem directing the search. In active surveillance, the goal is to find a specific technology to solve a specific problem.

Passive surveillance moves into an active phase as a particular technology becomes known to the company. The individuals doing surveillance bring the technology to the attention of their user community, and the user managers decide to pursue it or not. Individual technologies are moved into an active surveillance phase when a decision to pursue is made.

Company size is irrelevant to the need for surveillance, but the smaller the company, in general, the more passive the surveillance usually becomes, owing to the skills and effort required to conduct sophisticated, active surveillance. Large companies like Mobil Oil and JC Penney typically do both types of surveillance. Because of the complexity of the technology and its importance to the firm, these companies are likely to have one or more people whose jobs are devoted entirely to technology surveillance.

However surveillance is accomplished—actively or passively—use of a technology purely for its own sake may not add substantively to either the affect or the effect of a site. The challenge, then, is to identify innovative, value-adding technology applications that can meet the changing demands for Web site content, design, and hyperlinks.

Web Design in the Real World

Best Personalized Books

The prototype, first-generation, text-only application for Best was developed on disk and never went "live" on the Web. The text-only version was not acceptable to Jack and Wendy, who felt that to convey their image as competent, contemporary publishers, the Web site should use more sophisticated graphics and multimedia. As a result, the second-generation application was deployed as a live prototype. This second-generation version of the site is presented at http://www.cox.smu.edu/~sconger/bestwelcome1.html.

Currently, Sue and the team at Best are redesigning the Web site to be frame-based. Several factors led to this decision. One was that a greater percentage of browsers support frames. The second was that feedback on the site's navigation indicated that some users (from within Best) were not always sure which hyperlink to click. The frames design attempted to solve these problems.

The first frame is a menu bar down the left side of the screen. It not only contains a selection of hyperlinks, but also indicates user location within the site. This design provides the user with better navigational control, and, as a fixed element, gives the user a sense of continuity. Wendy's original idea of using a multicolor border to tie the site to print ads was also implemented as a bar on the menu frame. It loads only once

and does not hinder the load time of the other frame.

The second frame will contain the information from all of the other Best pages. There is less information on each individual detail frame, but the trade-off in making navigation easier was determined to be more important than the information display.

Mike Heischman, the computer specialist who attended some design meetings, was designated as Webmaster. He joined the team to participate in the frames-based design, estimating one to two days per week to be spent on Web surveillance, maintenance, and upgrading to the frames version.

In addition, Sue is on the Web daily for one or more hours. She searches for children's personalized books and prints competitors' pages for Jack, Wendy, and Mike to review. To give them easy access to these sites, Sue bookmarked them on a computer at Best's offices.

Jack, who has a master's degree in MIS, has begun to surf periodically himself but, like many new users, feels that wading through irrelevant pages to find the gems is more time consuming and less rewarding than he expected. He does look at competitors' pages and sites along with Wendy and Mike to decide on upgrades for their own site.

S u m m a r y

The World Wide Web changes every day as new technologies are developed and presenters, designers, and information stewards implement innovative new sites. For this reason a Web presentation is never completed. Dedication to maintenance and improvement is a must on the part of everyone: stewards, designers, presenters, and Webmasters. The organization must put in place adequate, permanent support for the site, both to keep the application running smoothly and to make necessary changes. Failure to provide such support after an application is implemented and goes live is a common problem.

Although all of the activities involved in monitoring the Web site are highly interrelated, they can be broken down into four basic categories:

1. The Web site's **content** must be reviewed for timeliness, completeness, and appropriateness for the organization's purposes.

2. The Web site's **design**, including its aesthetic appeal, should be reviewed. Once-fresh or trendy designs become dull and dated. For many presenters the relative importance of affectiveness changes after several months of experience with their Web site.

3. The Web site's **hyperlinks** must be reviewed frequently, especially intersite links. The destination points of intersite hyperlinks have a tendency to either disappear or change so radically that they no longer satisfy the purposes for which they were included.

4. Surveillance should continue to ensure that the Web site's **technology** platform is the best match, given new technological developments. Organizations may use either active or passive surveillance techniques or a combination of the two.

Each of these four types of maintenance demands that the organization reach outside itself for feedback and information about the site. For content, design, and linkages, this involves soliciting external user feedback of various forms. For technology, this involves reading periodicals, attending trade shows, meeting with vendors, and more to keep abreast of developments that might improve a Web presentation's effectiveness, affectiveness, or navigational efficiency.

R e v i e w   Q u e s t i o n s

1. Who should be assigned to Web site maintenance?

2. What factors influence the need for Web site design changes?

3. Why is it important to review hyperlinks regularly?

4. Name several developments that would prompt those people monitoring the Web site to update its information.

5. What are the different types of surveillance? What are the circumstances under which each should be used?

P r o j e c t s

1. Surf the Web to find the ugliest site you can. What are your criteria for choosing this site? What do you think was in the minds of the team that developed it? What process would you guess was used to develop the Web pages? Using the form from your instructor, evaluate the site for design, effect, affect, and navigational efficiency. Create a list of improvements you would make. Try to contact the site's Webmaster electronically and interview them to find out what the design process entailed.

C a s e   P r o j e c t

1. So far the case project assignments have focused on building a useful product. For a Web presentation to stay truly useful, however, it must fit into the organization for which it was designed. Where does your presentation fit into the organization's value chain? How important is the Web presentation in the organization's scheme of priorities? What actions should it take to ensure continued, effective use of your project?

2. Based on what you find, prepare a plan for identifying the needs and participants for creating succeeding generations of your presentation. If asked, develop a maintenance schedule for each page in the current presentation, identifying the volatility of the information and proposing a schedule for evaluating the addition of new threads and new user groups.

F u r t h e r   R e a d i n g

- Kruger, Richard A. *Focus Groups: A Practical Guide for Applied Research*. Thousand Oaks, Calif.: Sage Publications, 1991.

- Lefferts, Robert. *How to Prepare Charts and Graphs for Effective Reports*. New York: Harper-Row, 1881.

- Lindof, Thomas. *Qualitative Communication Research Methods*. Thousand Oaks, Calif.: Sage Publications, 1995.

- Martin, James, and Carma McClure. *Software Maintenance: The Problem and Its Solutions*. Englewood Cliffs, N.J.: Prentice-Hall, 1983.

- Morgan, David L., editor. *Successful Focus Groups: Advancing the State of the Art*. Thousand Oaks, Calif.: Sage Publications, 1993.

- Perrits, Henry H., Jr. *Law and the Information Superhighway: Privacy, Access, Intellectual Property, Commerce, Liability*. New York: John Wiley & Sons, 1996.

GLOSSARY

Accessed hyperlink A link that has been accessed—that is, the Web page at the other end of the link has been completely loaded—during the current Web session.

Active hyperlink A link that has been clicked and indicates that the linked Web page is still in the process of loading. Active links are sometimes indicated by a specific color that appears while the Web page is loading.

Active indexing One of the methods employed by search engines to compile Web site addresses. The search is directed by the user's desire to solve a particular problem with or add a new dimension to one's Web presentation. *See also* indexing and passive indexing.

Active surveillance The search for a new technology on the Web that is directed by the desire to solve a particular problem with or add a new dimension to one's Web presentation.

Affectiveness A measure of a Web presentation's emotional and/or aesthetic appeal. An affective presentation is interesting and stimulating, engaging the user's attention and encouraging further exploration of the site.

Alignment One of four principles determining the arrangement of information objects on a Web page. Alignment refers to the positioning of page elements relative to the edges of the page. Alignment may be left, right, or centered.

Alphabetical grouping A means of categorizing or grouping information objects, in this case alphabetically (as in the names on a guest list).

Applet A self-contained program, frequently embedded in HTML, that can be integrated into a Web presentation and launched to provide such effects as "live" interactive animation.

Associative relationship One of three kinds of relationships that can be shared by information objects. In this case, one that is based on the presenter's anticipation of relationships the user will need or want.

Atomic information object The smallest, most discrete form of information object. A unit of information that cannot be further divided without changing or losing its identity.

Available hyperlink A link that has not been used during the current Web session. Available links are indicated by a specific color; the color changes once the links have been used.

Boolean operators Words and symbols (such as "AND," "OR," and "+") used in combination with keywords to narrow a search for information on the Web.

Byte The unit of eight bits used to measure computer storage capacity. One byte is about the amount of computer memory needed to store one number or letter typed from a keyboard.

Cardinality A measure of how many different instances there are of a particular information object.

Chunks. *See* information objects.

Chunking The process of breaking down the information to be included in a Web presentation into discrete units called information objects, or chunks.

Closed-ended question A type of question that allows a narrow form of response, such as "yes" or "no," "true" or "false." Used in interviews during the development of a Web presentation to obtain or confirm specific information.

Closure A sense of completion a user should feel after traveling the complete length of a thread—that is, a sense that the purpose of pursuing that particular path has been fulfilled.

Contrast One of four principles determining the arrangement of information objects on a Web page. Contrast refers to the use of different design elements (such as color or typeface) to highlight differences (hyperlink text from regular text, high level of heading from lower one).

Critical linking object An information object that has links to many other information objects and is required for users to access and understand lower-level information.

Decoration One of four main purposes that multimedia can serve when added to a Web presentation. Decoration is a graphic adornment that is not strictly required for meeting the goals of the presentation but enhances its overall tone and affectiveness.

Demonstration One of four main purposes that multimedia can serve when added to a Web presentation. It involves the designer-controlled unfolding of a thread—that is, the user is presented with a certain sequence of "events" orchestrated by the designer.

Description One of four main purposes that multimedia can serve when added to a Web presentation. Descriptive multimedia elements improve on or clarify the information conveyed in the original text.

Designer The member of the Web presentation team responsible for coordinating all aspects of Web presentation development: gathering, compiling, and organizing information; executing visual design; and performing the technical tasks necessary to post the presentation on the World Wide Web.

Effectiveness A measure of a Web presentation's completeness and accuracy. An effective Web presentation contains all of the information, or content, a user might be expected to want given the purpose or focus of the site.

Exploration One of four main purposes that multimedia can serve when added to a Web presentation. It is the interactive, user-controlled unfolding of a thread. The user is free to choose among the objects presented for viewing such that he or she controls the experience.

Extranet An Internet-like, private network joining two or more business organizations with common interests.

Focal point The place on a Web page intended to draw the user's attention first. It is usually set off from the surrounding area through use of contrast.

Focus group A group of people brought together as a way to gauge public response to a particular product or service. For Web presentations, focus groups are used to help the presenting organization determine the overall effectiveness, affectiveness, and navigational efficiency of a Web presentation and improve it before the presentation goes on-line.

Frame An option for formatting Web pages that allows for the simultaneous display of several different pages, each functioning independently from the others.

Free hyperlink. *See* intersite hyperlink.

Functionality A measure of what the pages in a Web presentation will actually *do*—for instance, provide an e-mail address or accept orders for a specific product.

General-to-specific (gen-spec) relationship One of three kinds of relationships that can be shared by information objects—in this case, one that proceeds from general information to specific information to still more specific information.

Hit In a list of Web sites retrieved by a search engine, each individual entry, or site, is called a hit.

Home page The first page on a Web presentation.

Hyperlink The jumping-off point on a Web page from which a user can go to another hyperlink on the same Web page, on another page within the same Web site, or on another page within a different Web site. Each hyperlink has a distinct address, or URL, that allows the hyperlinks to "find" each other.

HyperText Markup Language (HTML) A language, or code, embedded in Web pages that formats their content for display on a computer screen.

HyperText Transport Protocol (HTTP) The standard for communication that governs the transfer, or movement, of objects on the Web.

Icon A visual, sometimes universal shorthand used to quickly communicate an idea, event, or subject. The stop sign, for instance, is the universal icon that communicates the instruction "Stop!"

Indexing The method used by search engines to compile Web site addresses. *See also* active indexing and passive indexing.

Information decomposition The initial process of breaking down all of the information being considered for the Web presentation into discrete units, or information objects.

Information domain The totality of the information provided in a Web presentation. It defines what information is to be included and what information is to be excluded.

Information object A fully-defined unit of information that is the basis for each element in a Web page. Each information object (also called a chunk) eventually results in a Web page element.

Information steward A member of the Web presentation team who is responsible for the accuracy of the information on the site and its appropriateness for expected users.

Information structure diagram A diagram developed from an outline of information objects that is the first representation of how they will be arranged on the Web presentation; it lays out the objects in relation to one another.

Information structuring The process of regrouping and reorganizing information for purposes of presentation on the Web after it has been broken down into discrete units, or information objects.

Information-centered analysis An approach to defining the information domain that focuses on the categories of information to be included in a Web presentation.

Intelligent agent software A program that searches through archives or other information repositories (such as the Web) on a topic specified by a user. Also called a spider.

Internet A huge network of computers allowing users around the world to exchange information and resources.

Intersite hyperlink A hyperlink that when accessed brings the user to a different hyperlink in a different Web presentation. Also called a free hyperlink.

Interview *See* structured interview and unstructured interview.

Intranet An Internet-like network that is internal to an organization and can be accessed only by members (or employees) of that organization.

Intrapage hyperlink A hyperlink that when accessed brings the user to a different hyperlink on the same Web page.

Intrasite hyperlink A hyperlink that when accessed brings the user to a different hyperlink on a different Web page within the same presentation.

Is-a relationship One of three kinds of relationships that can be shared by information objects—in this case, one in which a particular object *is-a* representative of a larger, more general group of objects.

Keyword A word a person submits to a search engine to narrow the search for the information desired.

Layout The arrangement of information objects on a Web page.

Load time In Web presentations, the amount of time required to display a Web page in its entirety once it has been accessed through a hyperlink.

Location grouping A means of categorizing or grouping information objects, in this case according to an object's relative position in a larger grid or system of organization.

Map An option for formatting Web pages that lays out hyperlinks over a map-like graphic.

Menu An option for formatting Web pages in which hyperlinks are arranged in a list for selection by the user.

Multimedia Communications media (including text, graphics, sound, animation, video, and more) combined for use in a single product or Web presentation.

Navigational efficiency A measure of the ease with which a user can progress through a Web presentation and access the information he or she wants.

Network Two or more computers connected together for the purpose of sharing information and resources.

Object relationship matrix A spreadsheet-like matrix used in structuring information that depicts each and every linkage from one information object to another, to show the extent of interconnectedness of the proposed Web presentation.

Open-ended question A type of question that demands no specific answer (such as "yes" or "no") but encourages a broad, wide-ranging response. Used in interviews conducted to help determine the information domain during the development of a Web presentation and to evaluate the responses to a presentation once it is ready to go on-line.

Passive indexing One of the methods employed by a search engine to compile Web site addresses. The search engine simply accepts addresses submitted by managers of other Web sites.

Passive surveillance The casual observation of trends, competitors' activities, new technologies, and the like that *may* be of significance to an organization and its Web presentation.

Presenter The organization sponsoring a Web presentation or the member(s) of the Web presentation team with ultimate decision-making authority over the content of and resources allocated to the site.

Presenter-defined grouping A means of categorizing or grouping information objects, in this case according to some attribute that the presenter assumes will be valuable to users.

Prototype The most recent working version of the Web presentation. Depending on what stage of development the presentation is in, the prototype could be an outline, a storyboard, or even an early onscreen version of the site.

Proximity One of four principles determining the arrangement of information objects on a Web page. Refers to the practice of placing information objects that contain similar or related information near each other.

Push technology A software program that automatically sends Web information to a user's terminal.

Quantitative grouping A means of categorizing or grouping information objects, in this case according to quantity.

Repetition One of four principles determining the arrangement of information objects on a Web page. The practice of using a design element (such as an icon or shade of color) more than once so that users associate it with a particular function (an icon of a shopping cart to indicate that a purchase can be made, a shade of color to indicate an available hyperlink), a particular topic (mystery books), or even a particular Web site (a decorative motif repeated on each page).

Search engine A software program that helps a user search for and locate specified keywords on the Web by listing Web sites that may contain the relevant words. Each site listed is referred to as a hit.

7 ± 2 rule A rule of thumb suggesting that, on average, people are able to deal with (or mentally process) only five to nine (hence 7 ± 2) concepts at one time. To be used as a guideline for breaking down information in a Web presentation, presenting information on a page, and developing hyperlinks.

Storyboard A display of pictures and text representing each information object as well as all linkages, cardinality, and volatility. Used during Web presentation development to get a better feel for how the presentation will look and function.

Structured interview An interview in which the interviewer asks the same set of questions to every person interviewed on a certain topic.

Surfer One of the millions of people who access the World Wide Web and the Internet to see what they have to offer. (Compare to user.)

Technology surveillance Performed for the purpose of improving on a Web presentation, technology surveillance is the ongoing observation and evaluation of new technologies from the time they are announced until they are mature enough to be incorporated into a Web presentation. *See also* active surveillance and passive surveillance.

Thread The path a user travels in moving from one hyperlink to the next.

Time grouping A means of categorizing or grouping information objects, in this case chronologically.

Typeface Any of the hundreds of families of type characterized by a distinctive and consistent style. Examples include Times Roman, Helvetica, and Garamond.

Type style Italic, boldface, small capitals, etc.—each is a type style that can be applied to any typeface for visual effect.

Uniform Resource Locator (URL) An address that specifies where on the Internet a particular resource is stored. Each Web page has its own URL, as do hyperlinked multimedia.

Unstructured interview An interview that proceeds somewhat spontaneously as the interviewer frames questions based on the various responses of the interviewee.

User A person with a decided interest in a Web presentation and who uses it to access, acquire, or act on the information available there. (Compare to surfer.)

User-centered analysis An approach to defining the information domain that focuses on expected user groups and the information or resources they are likely to want from the Web presentation.

Virtual value chain analysis A method of data collection in which the process used to provide a service or create and sell a product is analyzed to determine what aspects of that process could be used with success on a Web presentation.

Volatility A measure of the frequency with which an information object requires updating.

Web browser A software program that enables the user to view and navigate documents on the Web.

Web document. *See* Web page.

Webmaster The person assigned to the upkeep of a Web presentation once it is on-line. Responsibilities include monitoring the overall functioning of the presentation, responding to e-mail, and forwarding requests for information to the appropriate person or department.

Web page A single document within a particular Web site. Each Web page in a site is distinguished and can be located by a unique address know as a Uniform Resource Locator (URL).

Web presentation A related set of Web pages. *See also* Web site.

Web server An intermediary computer that provides access to the information and resources on the World Wide Web and can host, store, and provide access to Web sites.

Web session The period of time during which a user is "on the Web." It begins when Web browser software is initiated and ends when it is closed.

Web site A related set of Web pages (also called a Web presentation) or several different sets of Web pages (or presentations) stored on the same Web server.

World Wide Web (WWW) A huge collection of documents connected electronically over the Internet by means of a special language called HyperText Transfer Protocol (HTTP). Also referred to as the Web.

INDEX